The **Young Citizen'**
been produced by
Foundation, an
educational charity
empower individua
the wider comm
education about the law,
democracy and society.

The Citizenship Foundation,
Ferroners House,Shaftesbury Place,
(off Aldersgate Street)
London EC2Y 8AA

Tel 020 7367 0500
Fax 020 7367 0501

www.citizenshipfoundation.org.uk

Email
info@citizenshipfoundation.org.uk

Charity Reg. No. 801360

website support is available for
all those using this guide as a
teaching and learning resource,
www.teachcitizenship.co.uk.

INDIVIDUALS
ENGAGING IN
SOCIETY

Citizenship Foundation

The Citizenship Foundation would like to thank Hodder and Stoughton Educational for their support in the production of this ninth edition.

We would also like to thank the **Law Society Charity** for their continued support for this and other projects.

Editor and main author Tony Thorpe

Concept devised by Andrew Phillips, Lord Phillips of Sudbury OBE, President of the Citizenship Foundation.

We would like to thank Dan Mace, Kathleen Bennett, Shula Maibaum, Amy Bush, Janany Kathirgamanathan and Fiona Hogarth at the Citizenship Foundation.

Also lawyers at Allen & Overy, Linklaters, Lovells, and White & Case for their help in updating the law in this edition.

Designed and illustrated by Nomad Graphique; Mike Gibas, Lena Whitaker, Laura Emms, Mark Askam and Adam Williams.

Photographs AbleStock, PhotoDisc, PhotoAlto, Nomad Graphique, Ingram Publishing, Metropolitan Police Service

British Library Cataloguing in Publication Data
A catalogue record for this title is available from the British Library

ISBN   0340 814853
First published 1994
Ninth Edition 2004

Impression number   10   9   8   7   6   5   4   3   2   1
Year   2007 2006 2005 2004

Printed in Dubai for Hodder & Stoughton Educational, a division of Hodder Headline Ltd, 338 Euston Road, London NW1 3BH.

life

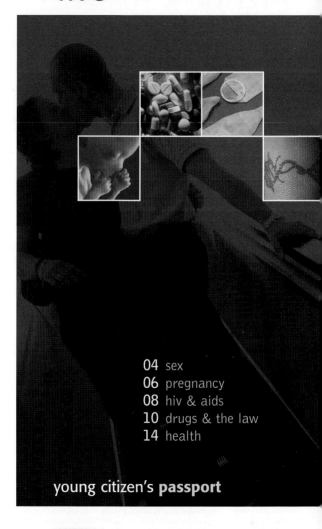

young citizen's **passport**

INDIVIDUALS ENGAGING IN SOCIETY

Citizenship Foundation

sex

Not the whole story

Although sex is discussed much more now than it was in the past, most people at some stage in their lives get confused about what they should and should not be doing. Probably the best advice is:

- **don't believe everything you hear,**
- **decide what feels right for you,**
- **talk to your partner and think about their point of view.**

You don't have to do anything that you are not comfortable with. Nor should you expect your partner to. There is no golden age by which you should have had sex. Some people will choose not to because they are not interested, or because there hasn't yet been the right opportunity, or because they want to wait until they are married. There's plenty of time and it's OK to opt out. Pressurising someone into going further than they want, as well as being morally wrong, can reach a stage where it is also against the law. For example, even kissing or touching someone without their agreement can be an assault. In law, both people must agree to what they are doing (known as consent), and they must understand what is happening. The person who gets someone drunk in order to go to bed with them, or takes advantage of their drunken state, risks being charged with rape. (See **safety**, page 21)

Sex and girls

Age of consent

A girl must be sixteen before she can legally have sex with a boy. If she has sex before this, her male partner is breaking the law. Girls, unlike boys, cannot be prosecuted for having sex under the age of 16.

The law doesn't usually get involved in punishing girls or women for having sex, although under the *Sexual Offences Act 1956*, a woman who has sex with a boy who is under 16 can be prosecuted for indecent assault, even if he consents.

Sex and boys

Unlawful sex

It is an offence for a boy or a man to have sex with a girl under 16 - even if she agrees.

If the girl is under 13, the maximum penalty is life imprisonment, since a girl of 12 or under is assumed by the law not to understand the consequences of having sex. A man who has sex with a girl aged 13-15 can be given a prison sentence of up to two years. A man aged 24 or over has no defence and will be found guilty. If he is under 24,

use the law with care try talking first

has never been charged with the same offence, and can show he genuinely believed the girl was 16 or over, he may be found not guilty.

A boy aged ten or over can be prosecuted for having sex with a girl who is under 13, and it's no defence for the boy to say in court that the girl agreed.

Lesbian and gay relationships

For women

Lesbian relationships are lawful. The law says nothing about lesbianism in general.

For men

Gay relationships are lawful if both men consent, are 16 or over and act in private.

For all

There are still difficulties for lesbian and gay people in a society where some people and faiths don't fully recognise a person's right to a gay relationship.

A change in the law in December 2003 protects people from discrimination at work on the basis of their sexuality (See **work and training** page 42).

If you need to talk to someone who understands, see **contacts** for groups who may be able to help.

Contraception

Each person who has sex is responsible for guarding against the risks to both people. It is important to know how to use contraceptives properly and how they affect your body. Good advice is therefore vital. For this you can go to a family planning clinic, your doctor or a Brook Advisory Centre. If you're under 16, a doctor can prescribe contraceptives for you without telling your parents - as long as the doctor believes that you are mature enough to understand what is being proposed. Condoms can easily be bought from supermarkets, garages, chemists, from slot machines in toilets and by mail order. Femidoms, which are a form of sheath for women, are sold in chemists. Both these and condoms are available free from family planning clinics.

Emergency contraception is also available to women who are 16 or over to prevent pregnancy up to 72 hours after unprotected sex or contraceptive failure. This is available from chemists without prescription.

The British Pregnancy Advisory Service now prescribes the morning after pill in advance of need, see **contacts**.

You think you're pregnant

Your period is late and you think you might be pregnant. What do you do? To find out if you are expecting a baby, you can ....

- **see your doctor;**
- **buy a pregnancy testing kit from a chemist. These are generally accurate and cost between £8-£10;**
- **visit a family planning clinic or a Brook Advisory Centre, who will offer confidential advice and provide a free test with an immediate result.**

What if it's positive?

You will have three choices: to go through with the pregnancy and bring up your child; to give the baby over to be adopted; or to have an abortion and terminate the pregnancy.

None of these may be wholly right - just the best in the circumstances. It is vital that you do everything possible to make the right decision for much hangs upon it, and the consequences can last two lifetimes. So talk, if you can, to your partner in the pregnancy, your parents, good friends, and your doctor.

Adoption

Giving up a baby for adoption is not easy - for the mother or father. It's best to talk to someone, such as your doctor or someone at the antenatal clinic, as soon as possible.

The adoption will probably be handled by a social worker who will discuss the kind of family the birth parents want their child to grow up in and will try to find out as much as possible about the birth family to pass on to the adopters. Adopters usually have to be married, but there are proposals to allow unmarried couples to adopt if they can provide a suitable home.

When the child has settled down with the new family, the adoptive parents can apply to the adoption centre at the local county court for an adoption order, which will be granted if the court is satisfied that all is well.

Neither birth parent has the right to see their child after she or he has been adopted, although the court can give permission for contact and the child can get in touch with them after they are 18. Help and advice for anyone thinking of having their child adopted is available through the British Agencies for Adoption and Fostering, see **contacts**.

use the law with care try talking first

ABORTION

The question of whether a person should have an abortion has serious moral and practical consequences. Those who are totally opposed to abortion believe that the unborn baby has a right to life in all (or almost all) circumstances. For others, however, it is the situation and feelings of the mother that should determine the best course of action. For anyone thinking of having an abortion it is almost always helpful to talk to someone about it. This can be a doctor, staff at the local family planning clinic or one of the other organisations listed in contacts.

Abortion in England and Wales is legal as long as it follows the law set out in the *Abortion Act 1967*.

This states that an abortion may be legally carried out if two doctors agree that:

- continuing the pregnancy would risk the life of the mother; or
- the mother is less than 24 weeks pregnant and continuation would risk injury to her physical or mental health or that of her other children; or
- there is a substantial risk that the child will be born severely handicapped.

Concern over the mother's mental health is a common reason for doctors to allow an abortion – particularly if they feel she is likely to suffer excessive emotional strain.

An abortion must by law, except in a few extreme cases, be carried out before the twenty fourth week of pregnancy. Anyone wanting to have an abortion using the National Health Service will need to start making the arrangements before the twelfth week.

If you are under 16, your parents must give their consent to end the pregnancy, unless two doctors decide that you are mature enough to understand what the decision really means. Doctors normally insist on having a parent's consent before giving a young person a general anaesthetic. An abortion can take place without anaesthetic, through tablets. But these are normally used only within the first eight weeks of a pregnancy.

The father, whether he is married to the mother or not, has no right to prevent her from having a legal abortion.

A doctor does not have to carry out an abortion if it is against his or her conscience. If this happens, you can arrange to see another doctor.

hiv and aids

What is HIV?

To understand HIV - standing for human immunodeficiency virus - you have to know something about the immune system that stops us from getting ill.

Blood plays an important part in our body's defence against illness. It contains millions of cells, about one per cent of which are white. A particularly important type of white cell is called the t-helper cell, and one of the jobs of these cells is to fight off infection.

HIV is a virus that attacks the t-helper cells. If it grows inside these cells, and other germs get into our body, we have no way of fighting infection. We become ill and develop what is called acquired immune deficiency syndrome, known as AIDS.

At the moment it is not clear whether everyone who is infected by HIV goes on to develop AIDS.

How do you get HIV?

Let's start with **how you don't get it.** As the virus dies quickly once outside the body, you don't get HIV from

• **hugging • kissing, including French kisses • sharing towels or cutlery • swimming • toilet seats • sharing musical instruments • giving blood.**

The HIV virus is found in the blood, semen, or vaginal fluid of a person with HIV or AIDS. Infection takes place when these fluids pass from an infected person into the bloodstream of someone else. This can happen in several ways:

• **by having unprotected sex with someone who already has the HIV virus. This means putting a penis into a vagina or anus without using a condom. The risk of contracting HIV infection through unprotected oral sex is thought to be much lower - but transmission is possible if semen, vaginal fluid, or menstrual blood come into contact with bleeding gums or mouth infections. You can help to protect yourself from HIV infection through sex by using a condom**

• **by using or sharing a hypodermic needle, which has already been used by someone with HIV, leading to the exchange of a small amount of infected blood**

• **as a result of a mother with HIV passing it on to her baby whilst it is growing inside her.**

Blood transfusions in industrialised countries should be safe as the blood used is routinely screened.

Anyone who feels they may be at risk of HIV or AIDS should seek medical advice and help, see **contacts**.

use the law with care try talking first

SEXUALLY TRANSMITTED INFECTIONS (STI)

Sexually transmitted infections (also called venereal disease, VD or the clap) are caught from sexual contact with people who have the infection themselves. Most STIs can be cured if treated as soon as possible, and so if you have had sex and you have sores or pain around your sexual organs, see a doctor straightaway. Don't have sex with anyone until it's cleared up, because you will put your partner's health at risk too.

However, not all STIs show signs of infection. Anyone who has sex with someone who is not their regular partner is at risk, particularly if they fail to use a condom. Chlamydia, for example, can pass undetected for some time, but may eventually produce pain and discomfort, and cause infertility in men and give women problems in conceiving.

Advice and treatment on sexually transmitted infections is available from clinics dealing with family planning, pregnancy or genito-urinary medicine, as well as family doctors. It is entirely confidential, although if you are under 16, the doctor may be reluctant to do anything without consulting your parents. If this is the case, it is worth checking first.

HIV and work

If you have HIV or AIDS, you are under no obligation to tell your employer. However, the government advises any health care worker who believes themselves to be at risk from infection to seek medical advice immediately. Your employer has a legal duty to treat the information that you are HIV positive as confidential. As a rule, employers are not entitled to tell other workers that an employee is infected with HIV, without his or her permission.

Employers may, if they wish, ask all those who apply for a job to take an HIV test. They cannot insist on existing employees taking a test, unless it is already in their contract. But if you apply for a job and the firm discovers that you are HIV positive they are quite within their rights to turn you down. If you lie about it, and they realise you are HIV positive after you have begun work, you may be dismissed.

If you are worried about HIV or AIDS, support and help is available, see **contacts**.

Prostitution

Prostitutes sell sex for money. They can be either men or women. It is an offence for a prostitute to attract "business" in public (called importuning) and for a man to try to obtain the services of a prostitute from a motor vehicle that he is in, or has just got out of. Prostitutes also risk physical abuse, sexually transmitted diseases, HIV or AIDS and pregnancy.

If the police become aware that a young person under the age of 18 is involved in prostitution, they will almost certainly inform Social Services who will decide whether to apply for an order to take that person into care.

drugs and the law

Controlled drugs

All drugs produce some kind of change in the way a person's body or mind works, and the availability of most drugs - whether aspirins, alcohol or amphetamines - is controlled by law.

The main law covering the use of dangerous drugs in Britain is the *Misuse of Drugs Act 1971*. Under this Act, drugs that people might misuse have been placed on a list of controlled drugs, and it is an offence to possess, produce or supply anyone with them. The list of controlled drugs is divided into three categories - Classes A, B and C.

CLASS A DRUGS

Cocaine is a white powder sometimes injected, but usually snorted, through a tube. Crack is cocaine treated with chemicals, so it can be smoked. Both give a high, followed by a rapid down. The only way to maintain the high is to keep taking the drug - but regular use leads to sickness, sleeplessness, weight loss, and addiction.

Heroin is made from the opium poppy - smoked, sniffed or injected. It comes as a white powder when pure. Street heroin is usually brownish white. Heroin slows down the brain and, at first, gives a feeling of total relaxation. Repeated use creates dependency. Overdosing causes unconsciousness and often death - particularly if used with other drugs, such as alcohol.

CLASS B DRUGS

Amphetamines sold as pills or powder, were developed to treat depression. They give a feeling of energy and confidence, but increasing doses are needed to keep up the effect. The downside is anxiety, insomnia, irritability and less resistance to disease and, as with all illegal drugs, there is no guarantee that they do not contain other harmful substances.

Barbiturates are used in medicine to help people who cannot sleep. They produce feelings of drowsiness and relief from anxiety. Sold as a powder or coloured capsule. Regular use creates dependency. Extremely dangerous when taken with alcohol or other drugs.

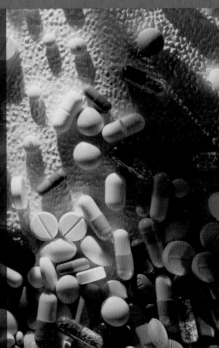

LSD, also known as acid, is a man-made substance, sold impregnated on blotting paper (often printed with cartoon characters or in colourful patterns) and dissolved on the tongue. It usually takes about an hour to work, and lasts up to 12 hours. The effects depend on the strength of the dose and the user's mood. It generally distorts feelings, vision and hearing, and bad trips lead to depression and panic, or worse, if the user is already anxious.

Ecstasy, or E, is sold as tablets of different shapes and colour. It makes the user feel friendly and full of energy, and sound and colours can seem much more intense. However, the comedown can leave the user tired and low - often for days. Regular users can have problems sleeping, and some women find it makes their periods heavier. Ecstasy affects the body's temperature control and it may cause the user to overheat and dehydrate. There is no guarantee that tablets sold as ecstasy do not contain some other ingredients. This can make their use unpredictable and dangerous.

Magic mushrooms contain hallucinogenic chemicals on the list of controlled drugs. It is not against the law to pick them fresh, but it is against the law to grow or prepare them in any way, or to possess them with the intention of supplying them to someone else. Most commonly used are the Liberty Cap and Fly Agaric. The effects are similar to a mild dose of LSD, with high blood pressure and possible stomach pains and vomiting. The greatest danger is in eating highly poisonous mushrooms, mistaking them for the hallucinogenic kind.

CLASS C DRUGS

Tranquillisers cause lower alertness, and affect people who drive or operate machinery. A number of anabolic steroids are also on the list of controlled drugs after concern over their misuse in sport and bodybuilding.

Although cannabis has recently been classified as a Class C drug, possession and supply remain illegal. Anyone over 18 found using cannabis is likely to receive a warning and to have the drug confiscated, but could be arrested if they are smoking in public or near a place where there are children. Those found repeatedly committing an offence are likely to face arrest and prosecution. Someone under 18 who is caught with cannabis, is likely to be arrested, taken to a police station and given a warning or reprimand. Their fingerprints and DNA will be taken and a record made. If it is not their first offence, they can expect to receive a final warning, or face a charge.

Cannabis comes in a solid dark lump, known as resin, or as dried leaves, called grass. The effects vary from one person to another. Some feel relaxed and happy, but the downside can be moodiness, anxiety, and difficulties with memory. Heavy users risk great tiredness, mental heath problems, and cancer - from the chemical constituents.

drugs and the law

The risks

• **There is no way of knowing exactly what is in drugs made or obtained illegally. This makes them unpredictable and dangerous.**

• **All drugs have side effects that may be dangerous and even fatal - particularly if they are mixed or taken regularly.**

• **Anyone using shared needles, filters or spoons, risks becoming infected with hepatitis or HIV, the virus that leads to AIDS.**

• **Employers and head teachers have a legal duty to confiscate drugs found at work or school and hand them to the police as quickly as possible.**

• **Illegal drug taking places a person's job, school, or college place at risk.**

• **A person prosecuted for illegal drug use will not necessarily be sent to prison, but could end up with a criminal record. However, a prison sentence is a strong possibility for someone found guilty of supply.**

Possession

Possession of a controlled drug is an offence, even if it's only a tiny amount. First-time offenders in possession of Class C drugs are likely to receive a reprimand or warning. Repeat offenders and users who smoke cannabis in public may be taken to court.

Supply

It is an offence under the *Misuse of Drugs Act 1971* to supply or to offer to supply someone with a controlled drug. Obviously this includes the sale of drugs - but it is still an offence even if money does not change hands. Giving a controlled drug to a friend or sharing a drug at a party by passing it from one person to another is still seen in law as supply. (See **leisure**, page 84)

It is also an offence if the substance sold is not actually a controlled drug, but the seller claimed or believed it to be one.

Production

It is an offence under the *Misuse of Drugs Act 1971* to produce any controlled drug. This includes letting someone use your kitchen or a room for this purpose.

Growing cannabis comes under this heading, and is an offence if you knew what you were doing.

▨ BRIEF CASE: Dennis

Dennis bought 1000 tabs of what he thought was LSD, and was caught by the police trying to sell them. When the tablets were analysed they were found not to contain LSD, but a harmless vegetable product that was not at all illegal. Despite this, Dennis was accused and found guilty of supplying an illegal or controlled drug, because his intention was to supply LSD.

Police powers

If a police officer has reasonable grounds to suspect that someone is in possession of a controlled drug, the officer can search that person and their vehicle and seize anything that seems to be evidence of an offence.

Glue sniffing

The effect of solvent abuse is rather like getting drunk on alcohol. However, it takes effect more quickly as the substances enter the bloodstream through the lungs rather than the stomach. Sniffers may experience hallucinations and, if plastic bags are used, may become unconscious or choke on their own vomit. Glue sniffing itself is not against the law, but it is an offence, under the *Intoxicating Substances (Supply) Act 1985* to supply a solvent to a young person under 18 if there is reasonable cause to believe that the fumes might be inhaled.

It is also an offence to sell lighter fuel to anyone under 18.

Tobacco and alcohol

Tobacco should not be sold by law to anyone who seems to be under the age of 16. Under the *Children and Young Persons (Protection from Tobacco) Act 1991*, shopkeepers can be fined up to £2,500 for selling tobacco or cigarettes to under age children. Police officers and uniformed park keepers have, in law, powers to confiscate smoking materials from anyone under 16 smoking in a public place. There has been some discussion about raising the age limit for tobacco sales to 18, but there are, as yet, no firm proposals to change the law.

For details of the law and alcohol, see **leisure**, pages 80-81 .

Information

Free publications on all drugs and solvents are available from most libraries. The National Drugs Helpline is open 24 hours a day, every day of the year, tel (free) 0800 77 66 00.

▨ BRIEF CASE: Alex

Alex was one of a group who bought and sold drugs for themselves and other students at their university. One day, his friend Paul took an overdose of heroin and died. It was Alex who had supplied the drug. A court sentenced him to five years in prison.

health

Doctors

Confidentiality

Once you're 16, you can decide about your own health care - although, strictly speaking, doctors don't need to consult parents of patients who are under 16, as long as they believe the patient fully understands what is being proposed. Patients also have a right of confidentiality. Nothing they say to their doctor should be passed on to anyone else - not even the fact that they made an appointment.

General practitioners

Everyone living in the UK, including visitors from overseas, is entitled to register with a GP. A list of local doctors is available from your local Health Authority, main post office, library, tourist information office, and Citizens Advice Bureau.

You have the right to change your GP at any time. You don't have to explain your reasons for doing so or tell the doctor concerned. However, a doctor does not have to accept you as a patient either. If you are refused in this way, the local Health Authority has a duty to give you details of local GPs within two working days. New patients are entitled to a health examination when they join a practice.

If you are staying for up to three months in another part of the United Kingdom, you can ask to be registered with another GP on a temporary basis. But if you are leaving home and going to college or university it's probably better to register with a new doctor in the town or city where you are staying, so you are guaranteed all the services of the practice if you ever need them. It's helpful to provide your medical card or National Health number when you register. If you don't have these, you will need to know your place of birth and the name and address of the doctor or practice with which you were previously registered.

PRESCRIPTIONS

Prescriptions are free if you:
* **are under 16 (24 in Wales);**
* **are under 19 and in full-time education;**
* **are pregnant or have had a baby in the last 12 months;**
* **suffer from a serious illness;**
* **or your partner receive Income Support, income-based Jobseeker's Allowance, Working Tax Credit or Child Tax Credit; or**
* **your name is on a current HC2 charges certificate.**

Further details are available from GPs, the Citizens Advice Bureau and from libraries.

Anyone now claiming a free prescription will be asked to provide proof that they are entitled to do so. A person who cannot do this should not be refused the prescription, but a check on their entitlement may be made by a prescription fraud team.

Records Your right to see your health records depends on when they were made. Subject to certain patient safety safeguards you can obtain all your records since 1991. If they are on computer you will be charged a fee of £10 under the *Data Protection Act 1998*. If you find the computer records are incorrect or misleading, you are entitled to apply to have the information altered or removed or to add your own version of events.

The *Access to Health Records Act 1990* gives you a right of access to health records kept on paper produced after 1 November 1991. Those made before that date can be seen if they are held on computer, but if they are handwritten, the decision is up to your doctor. The only reason your doctor can give for not letting you see records stored in your file after 1 November 1991 is that doing so would cause serious mental or physical harm to you or someone else.

DENTISTS

NHS dentists now operate a Community Dental Service. This includes a continuing care programme, requiring patients to attend for a checkup or treatment at least once every 15 months. Patients who do not keep in touch with their dentist over this period risk losing their entitlement to NHS care with that dentist. Once a dentist accepts a patient for continuing care, the patient must be provided with all the treatment necessary for dental health, on the NHS.

Before each course of treatment, you will receive a treatment plan, showing the work the dentist intends to carry out and what it will cost. The dentist may offer to treat you privately, but should not place pressure on you by implying that the treatment is not available on the NHS. You do not have to accept the treatment being offered.

If you wish to change your dentist, the local Health Authority or Citizens Advice Bureau can provide you with a list of NHS dentists. The Health Authority should, within five working days, be able to find you a dentist who can give you NHS treatment.

If you need emergency treatment, but are not registered for continuing care, you should contact a local NHS dentist to see if he or she is prepared to accept you on an emergency basis. If they can't, contact your local Health Authority, who should be able to find a dentist prepared to provide treatment.

Charges are made for most dental treatment. But dental treatment is free if you:

- **are under 16 or under 19 and still in full-time education;**
- **are pregnant or have had a baby within a year of starting treatment; or**
- **or your partner receive Income Support, income-based Jobseeker's Allowance, Working Tax Credit or Child Tax Credit; or**
- **your name is on a current HC2 charges certificate.**

If you don't qualify for free dental treatment or help with the cost, you must pay up to 80% of the cost, up to a maximum of £372 (October 2003).

Dentists can charge a patient who fails to keep an appointment or cancels at very short notice. The level of charge varies from one dentist to another.

health

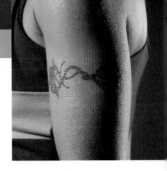

Opticians Eye tests are no longer free to everyone. You will get a free test if you:

- **are under 16 or under 19 and in full-time education;**
- **are partially sighted or need complex lenses; or**
- **or your partner receive Income Support, income-based Jobseeker's Allowance, Working Tax Credit or Child Tax Credit; or**
- **your name is on a current HC2 Charges certificate**

If you need glasses you may be entitled to help with buying them, particularly if you are unemployed or a student on a low income. Further information is available from opticians, the Citizens Advice Bureau and booklet HC11, *Help with health costs*, available from libraries.

Complaints If you have a complaint about the NHS or your treatment, it's important to make it as

soon as possible. Advice is available from NHS Direct, tel 0845 46 47.

Tattoos It's illegal for a person to be given a tattoo if they are under 18.

The right to die The law states that a doctor may give a patient a painkilling drug, which shortens their life, as long as the intention is to relieve pain and suffering and not to kill. If the drug is given with the intention of ending that person's life, the doctor can face a charge of murder.

It is possible to make what is called a living will (known in law as an advance directive) setting out how you would like to be treated if you ever lose the capacity to make or convey a decision. You must clearly understand what you are doing when you give the directive and, if it is done properly, it is legally binding on the doctor. But an advance directive cannot authorise a doctor to do anything unlawful.

Wills Anyone aged 18 or over can make a will, provided they are capable of understanding what they are doing. There is no lower age limit for people in the forces on active service, or sailors at sea.

Blood There's no legal minimum age to become a blood donor, but the National Blood Service won't accept anyone under 17. Donors usually give about three quarters of a pint twice a year.

safety

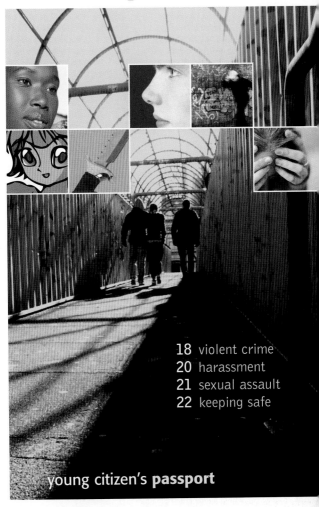

young citizen's **passport**

INDIVIDUALS ENGAGING IN SOCIETY

Citizenship Foundation

violent crime

Fighting Back

If you're threatened or hit, it's usually better to try to avoid a fight by talking to your attacker or backing off calmly.

If you can't do this, the law says that you can use reasonable force to defend yourself. This means that you're entitled to fight back, but not to go over the top and beat up the other person. If you do, you will have also committed an offence.

There is no law which says that you must report a crime to the police. If you want to claim compensation for your injuries the crime must first have been reported to the police.

Arrest – doing it yourself

If you see someone committing a serious offence or have reasonable grounds for believing that they have committed one, you can make a citizen's arrest. But, take care. People have been hurt and even killed trying to do their civic duty. The best advice is to take in as much as you can about the incident, and then to ring the police. If you do get involved, remember that an ordinary person only has the power to make an arrest for a serious offence - such as theft, serious assault, or burglary. Don't arrest someone for parking on a double yellow line.

Neighbourhood patrols also come up against this problem. They can't arrest someone who they think is about to commit an offence (it must already have been done), nor can they use excessive force - otherwise they can face charges of assault and wrongful arrest.

Victims of violent crime

Victims of violent crime can apply to the *Criminal Injuries Compensation Authority* for compensation for their injuries - which must be serious enough to receive an award. The crime must be reported to the police without delay, and an application for compensation made within two years of the incident that caused the injury. However, all cases are treated individually and an exception can be made if, for example, the delay in reporting was caused by the after effects of the crime.

Victim Support runs a helpline and advice to victims of crime. Their number is in the local phone book. See **contacts**.

If you are a victim of crime and called as a witness, you can arrange to see a courtroom before the case starts, have a seat reserved for someone accompanying you and ask to wait separately from other people. Details are given in the Victim's Charter and the Courts' Charter. See **contacts**.

■ BRIEF CASE: Raj

Raj ran an off-licence, and had twice been the victim of armed robbery. One night, a man carrying a long knife came into the shop demanding money from the till. As Raj was being held with a knife to his throat, his brother came through from the back and the robber ran off. Raj was so angry that he got into his van and chased the man down the street knocking him down and killing him. Raj was found guilty of manslaughter and sentenced to two and a half years imprisonment. The Court decided that he could not have been acting in self-defence because he was, by that time, not being attacked or threatened.

use the law with care **try talking first**

Self defence If you carry something to use for self-defence, you run the risk of actually breaking the law yourself. Under the *Prevention of Crime Act 1953*, it is an offence to carry something made, or adapted, to cause injury to someone. This includes things like a knife, bicycle chain, or a sharpened comb. The penalty is a prison sentence or a fine of up to £5,000.

Knives Under the *Criminal Justice Act 1988* and the *Offensive Weapons Act 1996*, it is an offence to have anything with a blade or sharp point in a public place. Folded pocket knives are allowed as long as the blade is less than 3" long. Schools are specifically mentioned as places where articles with blades or points must not be carried, and the police have the power to enter and search school premises if they have a good reason to believe that an offence of this kind has been committed. The penalty is a prison sentence or a fine.

SOME WORDS THEY USE

Assault & battery The word assault is not used in law in quite the same way as in everyday speech. Strictly speaking, an assault takes place when someone causes a person to fear that they are about to suffer immediate unlawful physical violence. Battery is the act of actually hitting that person or using force (even very little force) on them without their consent. Normally assault and battery take place at the same time. But it is possible to be assaulted without battery (raising an arm and shouting threats without hitting anyone), and to be battered without assault (hitting someone from behind without warning).

Burglary Burglary takes place when a person enters a building without permission, intending to steal, cause unlawful damage, seriously harm or rape someone. Even if nothing is taken or done, a crime has still been committed. It's enough in law to prove that the person intended to break the law in this way.

Robbery Stealing something with the use or threat of force.

Theft There are, in law, three parts to theft. A person is guilty of theft who
(i) dishonestly takes something, which
(ii) belongs to someone else, and
(iii) intends to deprive that person of it permanently.

young citizen's passport

harassment

Abusive behaviour Under the *Criminal Justice and Public Order Act 1994*, it is an offence to use abusive or insulting words or behaviour in public in a way that is intended to cause a person harassment, alarm, or distress. It's also an offence to put up a sign or a poster that is threatening or abusive in the same way. The law is designed to protect anyone who is being treated like this because, for example, of their race, disability or sexuality. Harassment of this kind is a crime - just like any other - and can be reported to the police, who have a duty to investigate and to try to find those responsible. Statements from witnesses will strengthen a case.

Punishment for offences that can be shown to be racially aggravated, such as harassment, assault and criminal damage now carry increased penalties under the *Crime and Disorder Act 1998*. Local councils also have a number of powers they can use to help tenants or homeowners in their area who are being racially harassed or attacked. They can prosecute residents for harassing or causing nuisance to other residents, they can get a court order stopping people committing certain types of anti-social behaviour, or, if those responsible are council tenants, they can evict them from their home.

The police or local authority can also apply for an anti-social behaviour order.

Stalking The *Protection from Harassment Act 1997* became law after a number of cases involving men following women over a considerable period of time. It is now an offence for someone to behave in a way that they know (or ought to know) amounts to harassment or puts a person in fear of violence being used against them. For an offence to be committed,

■ BRIEF CASE: Marcia

Marcia and her 10-year old son were not the only black people on their estate, but for some reason faced almost continuous trouble from one particular group of boys. Marcia first tried ignoring the problem and then spoke to the boys and tried to talk to their parents. Nothing worked. Eventually she complained to the council who investigated the case and obtained a court order requiring the parents of one of the boys to leave their house, which they rented from the council. The boy's parents appealed, saying it was not their offensive behaviour but that of their son. The appeal was dismissed. The judge said that Marcia and her son should not be deprived of their rights just because the parents could not control their son.

the behaviour or conduct must take place on at least two occasions and is punishable by imprisonment and/or a fine.

Someone who feels they might be a victim of harassment can apply to a court, for what is known as an injunction, ordering the person committing the offence to keep a certain distance from the victim's house or place of work. The victim can also apply for compensation for the worry they have suffered or for loss of earnings through time off work.

use the law with care **try talking first**

What if it happens to me? It all depends on the situation. If it's an isolated incident and the person is someone you don't know, then it may be best to try and ignore it. If you react and get abusive yourself, you run the risk of finding yourself in a far worse situation.

However, if it's happened before, or you're being harassed where you live, then it's important to tell the police - for your own safety. If you are getting abuse at school, college or at work, try and sort it out with the people concerned, but if that's not possible, or successful, raise it with someone in authority, who will have a legal duty to help you. See also the section on **discrimination** (page 41).

Someone suffering serious abuse or harassment may be able to claim compensation from the Criminal Injuries Compensation Authority (see page 18) and **contacts**.

sexual assault

Indecent assault Under the *Sexual Offences Act 1956*, it is an offence to touch or threaten a person in an indecent way. Groping and unwanted fondling can come into this category. Indecent assault carries a punishment of up to ten years' imprisonment.

Rape A male, over 10, who has either vaginal or anal intercourse with someone who doesn't want him to and who knows or doesn't care that this person is not consenting, commits the crime of rape. It's also an offence under the *Sexual Offences Act 1956* to threaten or force a person to have sex against their will, or to give them drugs in the hope that they will give in.

Going out with someone is not, in law, an invitation to have sexual intercourse with them. Forcing another person to have sex is rape, and it's no defence for the man to say that he was drunk.

It's also rape if the victim had too much alcohol or other drugs to know what they were doing. A wife doesn't have to have sex with her husband. If she does not consent, it's rape (see page 115).

If you are raped Although you may not want to tell anyone, most police stations now have women officers who have been trained to deal with victims of sexual offences in a sensitive way. If you are a woman, you can ask to be examined by a female doctor and you can take along your parents or a friend.

sexual assault

The police will be able to gather evidence more easily if you report the rape or assault as soon as possible. Reporting the crime early also makes your evidence more believable in court.

Once a victim tells the police that they have been raped or sexually assaulted, or the suspect has been charged, the victim has the right in law to remain anonymous. The victim cannot be questioned in court by the accused, nor can their name and address or picture be reported in the media. Attempted rape is dealt with in the same way.

Help is available from *Victim Support* and the local *Rape Crisis Centre*, who will talk to any girl or woman who has suffered an unpleasant sexual experience. *Survivors* offer an advice service for men. See **contacts**. Victims of rape can apply for compensation to the *Criminal Injuries Compensation Authority*. See **contacts**.

Male victims of rape are treated in law in the same way as female victims.

Accused of rape If you are accused of raping someone, immediately contact a solicitor. Rape is a serious crime, and the punishment can be severe.

keeping safe

There are some simple steps that both men and women can take to make themselves safer.

- **If you go out - especially at night - tell someone where you are going. If possible, stay away from known danger spots.**
- **If you're out late, get a lift back if you can with someone you trust, or book a taxi, see page 84.**
- **If you walk home, try to get someone to go with you.**
- **Check on the security of your home. Ordinary bolts and chains are not expensive.**
- **Knowing some self-defence can give you a feeling of greater confidence.**
- **If you carry a screech alarm keep it ready in your hand, not in your pocket or handbag.**
- **Men can help by taking care not to frighten women. For example, if you're walking in the same direction as a woman at night, don't walk behind her, cross over the road and walk on the other side.**
- **If you are facing some kind of harassment, tell someone about it. Ignoring it can make you more vulnerable.**

Abusive telephone calls It is an offence under the *Telecommunications Act 1984* to make malicious and threatening phone calls with a sentence of up to six months in prison and a fine of up to £5,000.

If you get such a call, try not to react and don't start talking to the caller. Don't hang up, but put the receiver down and walk away for a few minutes. Try to do something else, and then put the handset back without checking if the caller is still there. If the phone rings again, pick up the receiver and don't say anything - a genuine caller will speak first. Advice on dealing with calls of this kind is available from BT, tel free 0800 666 700.

CONTACTS see pages 134-143 for organisations able to give help & advice

education

young citizen's **passport**

INDIVIDUALS
ENGAGING IN
SOCIETY

Citizenship Foundation

attendance

Parents have the main responsibility, in law, for their child's education. Under the *Education Act 1996*, it is the duty of parents with children of compulsory school age, to make sure that their child has 'an efficient full-time education suitable to his age, ability and aptitude... by regular attendance at school or otherwise.'

The word 'otherwise' is important here because it allows parents to educate their children out of school. They do not need permission from the local authority, but parents must de-register their child if they are already in school.

Which school?

Under the *Education Act 1996*, parents can state a preference for the school they would like their child to attend, and the authorities must follow their preference if possible. But parents may be refused their choice if the school is full; is some distance from where they live; is a church school; or if the pupil has been expelled twice from schools already.

If admission to a particular school is refused, parents (but not pupils) have a right of appeal against the decision and should be told how to go about this in the letter of refusal.

Parents who cannot agree between themselves on a choice of school can ask a court to decide where their child will be educated. In this situation, the court must listen to and respect the wishes of the child concerned.

After their divorce, Peter's parents couldn't agree about where he should go to school. His mother wanted him to attend a boarding school, his father (with whom Peter lived) said that he couldn't afford the fees and felt Peter should go to a day school. Peter's mother asked a court to decide on her son's future education.

After hearing from both parents, the judge decided that Peter's father could well afford the school fees and so Peter should go to the boarding school. However his father appealed against this, saying that no one in court had asked Peter what he wanted.

The Court of Appeal did just this. Peter, who was 14, told the Court that he wanted to live with his father and couldn't do so if he was at boarding school. The Court of Appeal felt that it was important to take Peter's wishes into account, and said he could go to the school of his choice.

use the law with care try talking first

Costs

State education is free and it is unlawful for schools to try to make parents pay for books or equipment that pupils need for subjects or activities taken in school hours as part of the National Curriculum. However, charges may be made for…

- **individual music tuition;**
- **materials for practical subjects (if the pupil wants to keep the finished product);**
- **optional trips taken outside school hours;**
- **board and lodging on school trips, even if the activity is part of the school timetable.**

Parents who receive Disability Working Allowance, Family Credit, Income Support or income based Jobseeker's Allowance need not pay any of these charges.

The local education authority has a duty to provide pupils with free school transport or passes if their school is not within "walking distance" (for children aged eight and over this is three miles from their home) or where the route home is unsuitable, or it involves crossing a dangerous road. But this does not apply when the child has been offered a place in a suitable school that is closer, which the parents have turned down.

Pupils at school, below the age of 19, are entitled to free school meals if their parents receive Income Support or income-based Jobseeker's Allowance. Pupils who bring a packed lunch, must be provided with somewhere comfortable to eat it.

Leaving school or staying on

Under the *Education Act 1996*, compulsory school age begins in the first term after a child's fifth birthday. It ends on the last Friday in June of the school year in which they are sixteen. A parent cannot force their child who has passed compulsory school age to stay on at school against their wishes. Under the *Learning and Skills Act 2000* it is the duty of the Learning and Skills Council to provide educational opportunities for those over 16 (other than higher education). If your school or college can't offer the courses that you want, you should be offered a place elsewhere.

Students over 16 in full-time education whose parents are on a low income may be able to get an education maintenance allowance or an award from their local education authority. Details are available from your local education office.

Truancy

Parents have a legal duty to make sure that their child attends school regularly or is suitably educated elsewhere. If they fail to do this, they may be committing a criminal offence - and it is no defence for them to say that they didn't know their child was truanting or that they could do nothing to force them to attend.

To deal with this, the local education authority can require a family to work with an educational welfare officer to try to make sure that their child is properly educated. If this fails, or is not realistic, the parents may be prosecuted for a school attendance offence and imprisoned or fined up to £2,500. Under the *Crime and Disorder Act 1998*, a police officer who finds a child in a public place, may take that child back to school if the officer believes the child is of school age and is absent from school without permission.

rules & regulations

Religious worship and education

The *School Standards and Framework Act 1998* requires all pupils in state schools to take part each day in an act of collective worship that should be of a broadly Christian character . Parents can ask for their child to be excused. It is also possible for schools to apply to be allowed to provide non-Christian collective worship.

The law states that all pupils (including those between 16-18) should receive religious education as part of their curriculum. Again, parents may withdraw their child from these lessons and make alternative arrangements, but this must not interfere with the attendance of the pupil at school. Pupils cannot opt out of religious education or worship themselves; it must be done by their parents.

Sex education

The law states that all secondary schools must provide sex education for their pupils and in a way that recognises the moral issues involved. However, a parent can request that their child be excluded from receiving sex education and the school must comply with this request, except where it is part of the National Curriculum.

Schools can discuss questions of sexual orientation with pupils as long as it is done in a way (as it says in the *Education Act 1986*) that has 'due regard to moral considerations and the values of family life'.

Under the *Learning and Skills Act 2000* pupils must learn about the nature of marriage and its importance for family life and the bringing up of children.

Government guidelines encourage teachers to involve parents and other appropriate professionals if a pupil with a sexual or relationship problem asks them for help.

use the law with care try talking first

Punishment

Teachers are entitled to impose punishments - but these must be reasonable.

The *Education Act 1997* allows a school to keep a pupil under 18 in detention after school even though the pupil's parents may not agree. However, the detention must be reasonable in the circumstances and the pupil's parents must have been given at least 24 hours' notice of the detention in writing.

Pupils should not be held in detention for too long, nor should their safety be put at risk, eg if, as a consequence, they miss the last bus home.

Home-school agreement

Schools must, by law, ask all parents to sign a home-school agreement, listing the various things that they, the teachers and the pupil will do to improve that pupil's performance in school. Parents don't have to sign the contract if they don't agree with it and a pupil should never be refused entry because of this.

School uniform

Schools are entitled to insist that pupils wear a particular uniform, as long as it is reasonable and does not discriminate on grounds of sex or race. Pupils can be excluded from school if they persistently break the rules over uniform unless this is because of genuine religious or cultural reasons. Parents of pupils who are repeatedly sent home for not wearing the correct uniform may be prosecuted for failing to ensure their child regularly attends school.

Confiscation

Teachers may confiscate any forbidden items, such as mobile phones, jewellery etc, which they should keep safe and return to the pupil after a reasonable time.

If illegal drugs or weapons are found, teachers must confiscate the items and may hand them over to the police.

CORPORAL PUNISHMENT

Corporal punishment is now banned in schools throughout Britain – although there are circumstances, under the *Education Act 1996*, when a member of staff can use reasonable force to prevent a pupil from....

- committing an offence;
- injuring someone or damaging property; or
- behaving in a way that threatens the good order of the school.

However, if a teacher goes beyond what is reasonable, he or she may be have committed an assault, which can give rise to both criminal charges and a civil claim for damages.

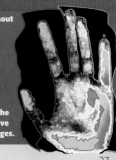

young citizen's **passport**

DRUGS IN SCHOOL

Schools are required to make clear to pupils and parents what action will be taken if pupils are found to be involved in any way with unauthorised drugs within the boundaries of the school. The term "unauthorised drugs" includes tobacco, alcohol, as well as illegal drugs, such as cannabis and cocaine, and the "boundaries of the school" may include journeys to and from school, work experience, and school trips.

The law allows school staff to take temporary possession of a substance suspected of being an illegal drug, but they are not allowed to carry out personal searches. Staff should persuade pupils to hand over any drugs voluntarily, and if a personal search is required, the police must be called to deal with the situation. However staff may search pupils' lockers or desks if they believe that drugs are stored there.

Government guidelines encourage schools to deal with cases individually and to take into account the circumstances surrounding each incident. Schools are almost always expected to tell parents of their child's involvement with illegal drugs.

Schools must make a full record of every incident involving unauthorised drugs, but have no legal obligation to report the matter to the police. The school's decision as to whether to inform the police will depend on the nature of the incident and what it sees as the interests of the pupil and the wider school community. If a headteacher decides to call the police, efforts must be made to contact the pupil's parents. The police should not interview anyone under the age of 17 without a parent, adult friend, or social worker being present.

Any pupil who has been involved with unauthorised drugs at school runs the risk of being excluded – either for a fixed period, or permanently. However, exclusion from school should not be automatic. The schools should first look for other ways of dealing with the pupil's behaviour and exclusion should normally take place only after a thorough investigation or when there is an immediate threat to the safety of other pupils in the school.

use the law with care **try talking first**

A student who breaks an important school rule or commits a criminal offence in school can be excluded from school by the Head, either for a fixed period of time or permanently. There is a national standard list of reasons for exclusions, which includes physical assault, verbal abuse, bullying, racist abuse, sexual misconduct, drug or alcohol abuse, damage, theft or persistent disruptive behaviour.

However, the decision to exclude a student should only be taken in response to a serious breach of school rules, and if allowing the pupil to remain in school would seriously harm the education or welfare of the pupil or others in the school.

It is important for Heads to carry out a proper investigation and to check, for example, whether the incident was caused by bullying, or racial or sexual harassment. One-off cases of truancy, lateness, forgetting homework, wearing jewellery, or breaking school uniform policy are not reasons for exclusion.

A fixed period exclusion is for a set length of time and fixed exclusions must not be for more than 45 school days in a school year.

When a pupil is excluded from school, their parents must be told without delay, and should receive a letter from the head explaining the reasons for the exclusion, how long it will last or if it's permanent, and how they can appeal against it. On appeal, the school governors can approve the exclusion or order reinstatement. A further appeal can be made to a local panel.

It's important to appeal as soon as possible - preferably within seven days of the exclusion. Parents are entitled to a copy of their child's education records and the school's discipline policy. The Government's guidelines on exclusion, called Guidance on Exclusion from Schools and Pupil Referral Units, are useful, as is advice from the Advisory Centre for Education. See **contacts**.

Only pupils or students over 18 have a right to be present at, or heard by, an appeal committee.

reports & records

A written report on a student's progress should be sent to parents at least once a year and a leaver's report should be given to every pupil when they leave school.

Under the *Data Protection Act 1998*, pupils of any age have the right to see their school records. They need to put their request in writing, but this can be turned down only if it is obvious to the head teacher that the pupil does not understand what he or she is asking for.

Parents also have the right to see their children's records, until their child reaches 18.

However the school can withhold certain items if it feels they might damage the mental or physical health of the pupil or someone else.

When a pupil transfers to a new school, head teachers must send all educational records to the new school.

If a pupil is refused permission to sit a public exam, eg GCSE or A level, his or her parents may appeal to the school governors against this decision. A pupil who has been entered for an exam but fails to sit it, without good reason, can be asked to pay the entry fee.

If a candidate does not do as well as expected in an exam, the school can ask for their paper to be checked, to make sure that the marks have been correctly assessed. Schools can also ask for a re-mark if it's felt that a serious mistake has been made in marking the paper. If the school remains dissatisfied, they can lodge an appeal with the Examinations Appeal Board. It is possible that compensation may be awarded if an examining board makes a serious error and this causes the student loss (for example, through deferral of a university place).

There is very little that can be done for a candidate who does badly in an exam because of poor teaching or a failure by a teacher to follow the correct procedure - or even the right syllabus. The examining board give grades based on the candidate's actual performance. Action through the courts for compensation would be extremely costly with no guarantee of success.

bullying

Schools have a legal duty to make sure students are safe in school, including on their journey to and from school. All schools must have an anti-bullying policy and policies protecting students from racial or sexual discrimination, and must act immediately on any evidence of a pupil being bullied. If they do not, they may be sued for negligence.

Schools are entitled to exclude pupils permanently who are persistent bullies and in serious cases may inform the police.

Childline provides a 24-hour telephone helpline, with trained counsellors able to talk to children and young people about bullying, tel 0800 1111.

Safety

Teachers take on some of the responsibilities of parents whilst pupils are in their care (known in law as being *in loco parentis*). On a school journey, this can apply for 24 hours a day. The standard of supervision required depends on the nature of the activity and the age or capability of the pupils. Where the action of teachers is called into question, the test the courts apply is whether they acted towards the pupils as careful parents would towards their own children.

■ Bullying

Ten pupils, who bullied younger children at a school in Doncaster, were found guilty of a total of 39 charges - including blackmail, robbery, and assault. The three most prominent members of the gang were sentenced to four, six and eight months in a young offender institution.

work
and training

young citizen's **passport**

INDIVIDUALS
ENGAGING IN
SOCIETY

Citizenship Foundation

part-time work

The law controlling the work of young people below school leaving age varies from one town or county to another.

Under the *Children and Young Persons Act 1933*, each local authority creates its own by-laws giving the terms and conditions for the employment of young people in that area.

These state the kind of work that a young person may, or may not, do and require employers to inform the council of all young people they employ. Although ignored in many areas, the rules also state that, generally speaking, anyone below school leaving age who has a part-time job must have a medical certificate of fitness for work and an employment card issued by the local council.

The only kinds of employment children under fourteen can be given are occasional light farm work, supervised by a parent, or parts in plays or films etc, for which a special licence is required from the local authority.

Children aged fourteen or over may be employed only in light work approved by their local authority.

No young person below school leaving age may be employed before 7am or after 7pm, for more than one hour before the start of school, for more than 12 hours a week during term time or for more than two hours on a school day, or on a Sunday.

A local authority licence is needed for someone between 14-16 to be paid to take part in sport.

There are few restrictions on the employment of 16 or 17 year olds. However, people under 18 cannot normally work in a bar, unless they work in a restaurant where drinks are served with meals, or are being trained for the licensing trade under a Modern Apprenticeship scheme. Copies of the by-laws controlling the employment of young people in your area can be obtained from the local library, or the council or education office.

A boy of 14, working in a factory making beds, suffered severe injuries when his arm was trapped in an unguarded machine. A court fined his employer £1,000 for failing to fit a guard to the machine and £200 for employing a child. The employer also paid £438 towards the costs of the case.

brief case

Employment rights

In 1994, senior judges decided that UK laws unfairly discriminated against part-time workers. As a result, many of the rights of those in part-time jobs (even if it's for only a couple of hours per week) are now the same as those of people in full-time employment.

If you are in part-time work you...

- are protected by the anti-discrimination laws, regardless of how many hours you work or how long you have worked for your employer;
- have the right, if you have worked for your employer for one month, to be given notice if asked to leave and, after two months to receive the terms and conditions of your job, in writing;
- are entitled to redundancy pay if you are made redundant and have worked for your employer for at least two years from the age of 18; and
- are entitled to claim for unfair dismissal if you have worked for your employer for at least a year, and feel you have been unfairly sacked.

The *Part-time Workers (Prevention of Less Favourable Treatment) Regulations 2000* state that part-timers must receive the same treatment as full-time workers in relation to their hourly rates of pay, training, holiday, and maternity rights, etc.

training

Youth training

A training programme place is guaranteed to anyone aged 16 or 17 not in full-time education or work and can be offered to those in work. Places are also available to anyone aged between 18 and 24 who has not received training because of ill health, disability, language problems, pregnancy or through being in prison or in care. No one can remain on youth training after their 25th birthday. There is no residential requirement for youth training. A young homeless person is eligible for a training place in the same way as anyone else in their age group.

The pattern for youth training varies. It can be full or part-time and a mixture of on and off the job training.

If you decide to train in the workplace you will probably choose between a Foundation or an Advanced Modern Apprenticeship. In a Foundation Apprenticeship, you will work towards a National Vocational Qualification (NVQ) at level 2 (equivalent to one A level) focusing on a particular skill e.g. information technology. You can go on to an Advanced Modern Apprenticeship and get an NVQ level 3 (equivalent to two A levels). Modern Apprenticeships are aimed at preparing for work at technician, craft or junior management level.

training

Connexions Card The Connexions Card, available free to all 16-19 year olds, is a smartcard on which you can collect reward points for learning, work-based training and voluntary activities. These can be exchanged for discounted and free goods. The card can also be used for discounts at outlets displaying the Connexions Card sticker. For more details, see www.connexionscard.com

Pay

You may be taken on as an employee or a work-based trainee. As an employee, you will receive at least the minimum wage. See page 38. Apprentices do not qualify for the minimum wage until they are 19 or have completed a year of their apprenticeship, whichever comes later. If you are a trainee, you will receive a training allowance, which can be reduced for part-time work or unauthorised absences.

Terms and conditions

Whether you are an employee or a work-based trainee, you are entitled to receive written details of the terms and conditions of your training. If you are employed you are covered by all the other rights and benefits mentioned in this chapter.

You will also be given an individual training plan that will explain:

- **how your training will be organised;**
- **the date when your programme begins and ends;**
- **your hours of work (if you are not employed, the maximum is 40 hours per week);**
- **details of the NVQ for which you are training.**

If you are not happy with your training, you may be able to transfer to a different programme with the same trainer or with another one. If your trainer cannot finish your training, you should be given the opportunity to transfer to another trainer with a similar training programme.

If you are absent for more than the period specified in your terms and conditions, without permission from your trainer, your training programme will end.

The Connexions Service, careers advisors, or your local Learning and Skills Council have details of apprenticeships in your area. Also see the Modern Apprenticeships website www.realworkrealpay.info.

use the law with care try talking first

BRIEF CASE: Karen

Karen applied for an apprenticeship at a garage in Surrey. She was the best qualified applicant and had already worked in a garage as part of her work experience. At her interview she was asked whether she minded spending all day in a pair of dirty overalls, covered in oil and grease. Karen said she wasn't bothered, but didn't get the job. Karen believed she had been unfairly discriminated against and took her case to an employment tribunal. The tribunal agreed and awarded just over £24,000 for loss of earnings and injury to her feelings.

Equal opportunities

Trainees have the same protection as other workers against unfair discrimination. Help is available at your careers office and the local Citizens Advice Bureau. For more information, see **equal rights**, page 41.

Health & safety

Your trainer or employer must make sure that the place where you work is safe, and you have a legal responsibility to follow all safety procedures and use equipment in the way instructed.

If you have an accident, or are worried about safety, speak to your supervisor immediately. If you are injured or become ill while training, you should also contact your local Jobcentre Plus. You should continue to receive your training allowance for three weeks after an accident and then you will need to make a claim for Income Support.

Anyone injured on a government funded training scheme may be able to claim Disablement Benefit. Contact your local Jobcentre Plus for details.

Problems

When you start training you should be told what to do if you have any problems while on the programme. If you are unhappy with the training you can discuss it with your supervisor or see the careers officer, who may be able to help solve the problem or find you more suitable training.

Non-employed trainees are not entitled to any notice if they are dismissed, nor can they take their case to an employment tribunal if they feel they have been sacked unfairly. But if they are offered another job, they don't need to work out their notice before leaving. Employed trainees or apprentices receive the same legal protection as other employees and should give whatever period of notice is stated in their contract of employment.

This programme is designed to help young people into work, with advice, support, training and work experience. It falls into two categories. The first is for people aged 18-24 who have been claiming Jobseeker's Allowance for six months or more. (Some people, such as lone parents, ex-offenders, those who have just left the armed services and those with a health condition or disability need not wait for the six month qualification period.) The second category is for long-term unemployed people, aged 25 and over.

New Deal for 18-24 year olds is compulsory in the sense that someone who doesn't take up the programme without good reason, stands to lose their right to benefits.

If you are eligible, you will have an appointment with a personal adviser who will explain the programme, give you advice on finding work and monitor progress, based on an action plan that you will be required to draw up. If, at the end of this initial period (up to four months) you are not yet in work, you will be given four options - a job for six months with an employer, work on an environmental project, work in the voluntary sector, or full-time education or training.

Again, if you don't accept any of these alternatives or fail to turn up to interviews without giving a good reason, payment of your Jobseeker's Allowance is put at risk.

If you choose the employment option, you have the same legal rights as other employees - but no right to remain in the post after six months. The New Deal expects employers to pay you the going rate for the job. Young people on the environmental or voluntary sector option receive a wage or an allowance equal to the Jobseeker's Allowance, plus £400 spread over six months and you will still get other benefits to which you are entitled.

The New Deal Information Line is on 0845 606 2626, open 24 hours a day. Specialist advisers are available Monday-Friday 9am-5pm.

applying for work

Applications

Read through the application form before starting to fill it in. Draft your longer answers in rough, until you are happy with what you have written.

All the information you give should be correct. An employer is entitled to dismiss someone who is deliberately misleading on their application form or at interview.

Your CV

Some adverts for jobs tell you to send for an application form, others will ask for a letter with your curriculum vitae, usually known as a C.V. This is something that you write or type, giving personal details, qualifications, experience, and interests. Make several copies and don't forget to keep one yourself.

use the law with care try talking first

Referees

You will need the names of two people who are prepared to act as your referees, to write a short report or reference about you for an employer. One referee is usually your last employer, or the head teacher or year tutor in your school.

Interviews

If you've not been to the office or building before, leave yourself extra time to find it; or go round and find out where it is beforehand. If you can't make the appointment, phone or write to explain and ask for a more convenient time.

Have a few questions ready to ask - about what the course or job involves. If they offer you a place or job, before you accept try to think if there's anything else you need to know. If there is, ask.

Everyone at work has a contract - whether full or part-time, permanent or fixed term.

A contract is another word for the agreement between you and your employer, spelling out the arrangements that will affect your work - such as pay, hours, the sort of job you will do, holidays and the notice you have to give, or you can expect to receive, when your employment comes to an end.

Terms and conditions in writing

If you are to be employed for more than one month, your employer must give you a written statement within two months of starting work, setting out the terms and conditions of your job.

This statement should give...

- **your job title and place of work;**
- **your starting date;**
- **your rate of pay, and details of how and when you will be paid;**
- **your hours of work;**
- **your holidays and holiday pay;**
- **arrangements for sick pay and pension;**
- **details of the firm's disciplinary procedures (only if 20 or more people are employed), and how complaints at work are dealt with; and**
- **the amount of notice that you or your employer must give if your contract is to be ended.**

contracts

People often think that contracts have to be written down - they don't. They can be agreed verbally - but it's a good idea to have things in writing, in case there's disagreement about what you're expected to do.

Check your contract carefully. Make sure you agree with what it says and that it covers everything you are being asked to do. If it is different from the agreement made at your interview, point this out. Keep safe all pay slips, letters and papers you are given by your employer.

Take care

If you agree to do something on a regular basis that is not written into your contract - like working on a Saturday - you may be, in law, agreeing to a new term or condition of work. If you decide later that working every Saturday is not a good idea, your boss may be entitled to insist that you continue. By turning up for work six days a week, you may have actually changed your contract by your conduct.

Pay

Your wages will either be agreed between you and your boss or else based on rates agreed between employers and the trade union. Either way, your employer must give you a detailed written pay statement each time you are paid, showing exactly what you are being paid and how much is being taken off in tax, national insurance etc. It is up to your employer to choose how you are paid. This can be by cash, cheque, or straight into your bank account.

Your rate of sick pay must be explained in your contract. It will probably say either that you will be paid at your standard rate for a certain length of time, or that you will be given statutory sick pay. This is set each year by the Department for Work and Pensions and is usually lower than your normal pay. If you are off sick for four or more days in a row (including Sundays and bank holidays) you will receive statutory sick pay from your employer for up to 28 weeks. You don't have to claim statutory sick pay, just follow your employer's rules for notifying sickness.

You can check what you should receive in leaflets available from Social Security offices and libraries.

MINIMUM PAY

The *National Minimum Wage Act 1998* sets minimum rates at which people aged18 or over should be paid.

The minimum rate payable to people aged 18-21 is £3.80 per hour and for people aged 22 and over, is £4.50 per hour, unless they are in the first six months of a new job or on an accredited training course. For more details, phone the Minimum Wage Helpline, tel 0845 6000 678.

use the law with care **try talking first**

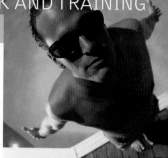

Hours

Your hours of work will normally be agreed between you and your employer, although there are some jobs where these are limited by law for reasons of health and safety.

The *Working Time Regulations* set a maximum working week of 48 hours, including overtime, calculated over 17 weeks for workers aged 19 and over. Workers who are 18 or under may not work more than 8 hours a day or 40 hours in a week. You can agree to do more than this, but your employer cannot pressurise you to do so. You are also entitled to:

• a rest break of 20 minutes when you work for more than 6 hours at a time (or 30 minutes every 4 hours if you are under 18);

• at least 11 consecutive hours off in any 24 hour period (12 hours off, if you are under 18). Workers who are 18 or under may not ordinarily work between 10pm and 6am. Some night work is allowed in certain jobs, such as the armed forces, farm work, catering, working in a pub, restaurant or hotel, working in a bakery, newspaper delivery

HOLIDAYS

The *Working Time Regulations* give most people over 16 the right to at least four weeks' paid holiday a year. During the first year of employment, you have the right to take one twelfth of your annual holiday entitlement for each month worked. Some jobs are not covered by the Regulations, for example those in the transport and fishing industries, the police, and armed forces.

and retail trading. However, an adult must supervise the work and rest periods must be given. Workers who believe that the hours they are expected to work do not follow the regulations, can take their case to an employment tribunal.

health & safety

Safety

Employers have a legal duty to take care of the safety of their staff. If they don't, they are breaking the *Health and Safety at Work Act 1974*.

This means that the equipment that you use must not be dangerous or defective, and that the people you work with must work safely and responsibly.

Your duty is to follow safety regulations and to take care of your own and other people's safety.

If you work for a firm where there are five or more employees, your boss must give you details of the health and safety arrangements in writing.

If you are worried about health and safety, raise the matter with your supervisor. Your employer may not dismiss you or treat you unfairly for raising genuine concerns, as long as you follow the right procedures. If you remain concerned, contact the local offices of the Health and Safety Executive. Your local Citizens Advice Bureau will be able to tell you how to do this.

health & safety

■ BRIEF CASE: Irene

Irene worked as a secretary in an office where several people smoked. Although a nonsmoker herself, she felt no ill effects as the area was well ventilated. However, when Irene's section was moved to another part of the building, with poorer ventilation, the smoke and smell started to become a problem. Despite Irene's complaints, her employer did nothing to discourage people from smoking or to create a better working environment. After nearly three years, Irene left the firm and found another job, but decided to take her case to an employment tribunal to claim unfair dismissal, saying she had been forced to leave because of her uncomfortable working conditions. The tribunal agreed - an employer has a duty to provide a working environment that is suitable for employees to work in.

Accidents

If you are injured at work, report the matter to your supervisor straightaway and, unless the injury is very small, see a doctor. Make a note of what happened, check to see whether you are entitled to any welfare benefits and get legal advice from either your trade union or a solicitor. You may be entitled to compensation for your injuries.

Using a computer screen

If you have a problem with your eyes that you think might be due to using display screen equipment at work, your employer has a duty to arrange for you to have an eyesight test if you ask for one, and to do whatever they reasonably can at work to reduce further problems. This is all part of a general requirement for employers to check on the health and safety risks to people using computer screens at work, contained in the *Health and Safety (Display Screen Equipment) Regulations 1992*.

■ BRIEF CASE: Gary

FINGER LICKING SAUSAGES

Gary, 18, worked in a butcher's and was cutting meat when his hand slipped and he cut off the top of two fingers. His boss had often told him to use a special guard - but most people at work ignored this, so Gary didn't bother either. Gary was awarded damages in court because his employer did not make sure that he was working in the right way, but they were reduced by a third because he hadn't followed the safety instructions.

use the law with care try talking first

Discrimination

It is against the law for an employer or training organisations to discriminate against someone because of their race, colour, country of origin, nationality, ethnic group, sex, marital status, disability or because they work part-time. See also page 42.

This is explained in a number of laws and regulations – the *Race Relations Act 1976, the Equal Pay Act 1970, the Sex Discrimination Act 1975, the Disability Discrimination Act 1995* and the *Part-time Workers (Prevention of Less Favourable Treatment) Regulations 2000.*

A few jobs are excluded from the sex discrimination laws. These include acting, modelling, and jobs involving physical or close contact with the opposite sex.

Direct & indirect discrimination

Not treating a person as well as someone else because of their skin colour, sex etc. is called **direct discrimination**.

Indirect discrimination is more subtle, and this occurs when conditions are laid down for a job that unfairly limit the chances of people from one sex, or a particular ethnic group. Both are unlawful.

Disability

The *Disability Discrimination Act 1995* protects certain groups of disabled people from unfair discrimination and applies to firms with 15 or more employees.

It is against the law to treat a person with a disability less favourably than someone without, unless it can be justified for a reason related to the disability. Employers are required to make reasonable adjustments to the working environment that would enable a person with disabilities to be employed.

■ BRIEF CASE: Eugene

Eugene suffered constant racist taunts from other workers on the building site where he worked, and the management did little to stop it. They said that "black bastard" and "nigger" were words often used on sites. The tribunal decided that Eugene had been directly discriminated against. He was awarded £2,000 damages.

■ BRIEF CASE: Susan

Susan, a train driver on London Underground, was forced to hand in her notice when new shift rosters meant that it was impossible for her to work and look after her three year old child. She took her case to an employment tribunal, complaining of sex discrimination. The tribunal decided that the new working arrangements indirectly discriminated against women because more women were single parents.

Other discrimination

From December 2003 the *Employment Equality (Religion or Belief) Regulations* and the *Employment Equality (Sexual Orientation) Regulations* protect people who face discrimination at work because of their sexuality, religion or beliefs. Transsexuals (people who have changed sex) are also protected from discrimination and harassment at work. Regulations against age discrimination are likely to come into force in December 2006.

Help and advice

If you feel you have been a victim of unfair discrimination at work, you can get help from your local Citizens Advice Bureau, Law Centre or trade union. Advice and information on racial matters is also available from the Commission for Racial Equality, on sex discrimination from the Equal Opportunities Commission and on disability matters from the Disability Rights Commission.

If you can't sort out things informally, you may be advised to take your complaint to an employment tribunal. This must be done within three months (or six months, if it is a claim under the *Equal Pay Act*). If you win, the tribunal can award damages to compensate you for the losses you have suffered. You may be able to settle your case without the need to go to court but, if not, be prepared for a long and difficult battle, and remember to take legal advice.

Unwelcome attention

Sexual harassment covers a whole range of things from rude remarks to leering and unwanted physical contact. They are known in law as direct discrimination, under the *Sex Discrimination Act 1975*. Although they usually apply to women, men can be victims too.

If you can, it's often better to try to sort things out personally. But if the harassment continues, don't be afraid to complain. It's not always easy to prove in court, but judges are now prepared to award damages when the victim can show that they have suffered some disadvantage or injury to their feelings from the sexual harassment.

■ BRIEF CASE

An employment tribunal decided that a secretary, who was sacked when she complained about being groped by a senior member of staff at a Christmas party, was unfairly dismissed. She was awarded £4,700 in damages.

use the law with care try talking first

maternity & family rights

All women at work who are expecting a baby have certain minimum legal rights. Some employers provide more than these. You can check your position from your contract.

Time off with pay for antenatal care

This applies to full and part-time workers, and it makes no difference how long you have worked for your employer. Your employer cannot insist that you make up the time, or that you take the appointment in your free time.

At least 26 weeks maternity leave

You are entitled to 26 weeks of ordinary maternity leave no matter how long you have worked for your employer, and whether you are full or part-time. An additional 26 weeks of maternity leave is available if you've worked for your employer for at least 26 weeks continuously by the fourteenth week before the child is due.

All benefits, except pay, listed in your contract, continue throughout the first 26 weeks of ordinary maternity leave – including medical insurance, pension, and even a company car, if you have one. Some benefits, such as statutory holidays, will continue throughout both the first 26 weeks of ordinary maternity leave and the 26 weeks of additional maternity leave.

Correct procedures If you don't follow the correct procedures in applying for maternity leave, you risk losing the right to return to your job after your baby is born. For example, you must give notice to your employer. The personnel department at work, your trade union, or local Citizens' Advice Bureau can explain what you need to do.

Maternity pay If you have been working for your employer for long enough, you are entitled to maternity pay for the first 26 weeks of ordinary maternity leave including the time you take off before your baby is born. This will probably be lower than your usual rate, unless it says otherwise in your contract. If you are on a low income or have not worked for long enough to qualify for maternity pay, you may still be entitled to a maternity allowance from the Benefits Agency. A guide to maternity rights is available free from the Department of Trade and Industry, see **contacts**.

The standard rate of maternity pay and the maternity allowance is £100 per week, or ninety per cent of your average weekly earnings, if less.

maternity & family rights

Paternity leave

Both parents have a right to take up to 13 weeks' unpaid parental leave over the first five years of their child's life provided they have worked for their employer for at least a year. During this time their job will be protected. The leave must be agreed with the employer. Unreasonable objections can be referred to an employment tribunal. Parents of disabled children are entitled to 18 weeks' unpaid leave over the first 18 years of the child's life.

Time off

Regardless of how long you have worked for your employer, you have the right to take unpaid time off for urgent family problems, such as an accident or sudden illness, but you must give your employer the reasons for your absence as soon as possible. You may only take a reasonable amount of time. If your employer refuses, you can complain to an employment tribunal.

Right to request flexible working

If you have 26 weeks' service and are a parent, stepparent, adopter, foster carer or guardian of a child who is under six years old or a disabled child who is under 18 years old, you have the right to request flexible working hours. Your employer can either agree or refuse your request. If you believe that your request has been refused unreasonably then you should complain, and if your employer does not follow the correct procedure you can refer your request to a tribunal.

trade unions

Membership

It is up to you whether you join a trade union. Trade unions don't only negotiate wages for their members. They also give advice, inform members of their rights and act on their behalf over difficulties with their employer. An employer must not sack someone for either belonging or not belonging to a trade union.

Not all employers want to work with unions. But, if there are more than 20 people working for an employer, a trade union may be able to force the employer to recognise the union and to negotiate with them.

Industrial action

If you take industrial action - for example, by stopping work - you may be breaking your contract. However, if the strike has been lawfully organised and correctly balloted, your employer is not entitled to dismiss you for taking part. This is automatically unfair and you may have a case for compensation. But you cannot claim unfair dismissal if you are sacked for taking part in an unofficial strike.

use the law with care **try talking first**

If you're sacked or made redundant, your legal rights mainly depend on how long you have been working for the firm.

Notice Unless you have done something very serious and committed what's known in law as gross misconduct - such as theft or fighting - your boss should not sack you on the spot. Your contract should state the notice to which you are entitled, and this usually depends on how long you have been working for your employer.

After one month's employment, either side should give one week's notice. After two years' employment, your employer should give you two weeks' notice, three weeks' after three years, and so on, up to twelve weeks' notice for employment which has lasted twelve years or more.

However, your notice period might be longer if this is stated in your contract, and your employer may decide to pay you instead of letting you work out your notice.

Reasons in writing If you are fired by your employer, for whom you have worked for more than one year, you can ask for a written statement of the reasons for your dismissal. Your employer must provide this within 14 days.

Redundancy This happens when an employer no longer needs the job done for which you were employed. Your rights mainly depend on your age and how long you have worked for the firm.

If you are made redundant, you have a right to redundancy pay, if you…

- **have worked for your employer for a continuous period of at least two years since you were 18;**
- **are under retirement age; and**
- **have not unreasonably turned down an offer of another job from your employer.**

If your employer has gone bust, you may be able to get a redundancy payment from the Redundancy Payments Service.

If you are made redundant, get advice from your trade union, Citizens Advice Bureau or a solicitor as soon as possible. If you feel that the way you were chosen for redundancy was unfair or unreasonable, you may also be able to claim unfair dismissal.

Information Your rights to a redundancy payment are explained in the Redundancy Payments Service Charter, available free from the Department of Trade and Industry. See **contacts**.

losing your job

UNFAIR DISMISSAL

If you feel that you have been unfairly dismissed, and have worked for your employer continuously for a year or more, you can make a complaint to an employment tribunal.

Even if you've not been sacked, but leave your job because of the behaviour of your employer, you may have a claim for unfair dismissal. This is known in law as constructive dismissal, but will only be successful if you can show that your employer has broken your employment contract. If you are thinking of resigning because of this, keep a record of what is happening and, before you hand in your notice, write to your employer explaining your reasons for leaving.

Take legal advice before you make a claim for unfair dismissal. Your trade union, local Citizens Advice Bureau or a solicitor can help. If you are unhappy about your dismissal, don't delay in seeking assistance. You only have three months in which to make a complaint.

If the tribunal agrees that your dismissal was unfair, your employer will probably be ordered to pay you a sum in compensation. This is based on the amount of redundancy you would be entitled to, plus a figure for compensation. The maximum basic redundancy award is £7,800 and the maximum figure for compensation is £53,500.

There are no limits to the damages you can receive if you lose your job through disability, race, or sex discrimination or if you are dismissed unfairly or selected for redundancy for reasons connected with health and safety matters.

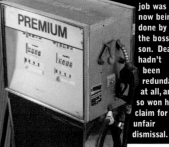

■ BRIEF CASE: Sacked!

Jeannette's son was ill in the night and Jeanette overslept the next morning. When she arrived late at the video rental company where she worked, she was sacked. She explained what had happened, but her boss took no notice. Jeannette took her case to an employment tribunal, who decided that she had been unfairly dismissed, as she had not been given a warning or a second chance.

■ BRIEF CASE: Redundant!

Business was bad and Dean was made redundant from his job at a petrol station. He was given £520 redundancy pay, but soon realised that his job was now being done by the boss's son. Dean hadn't been redundant at all, and so won his claim for unfair dismissal.

money

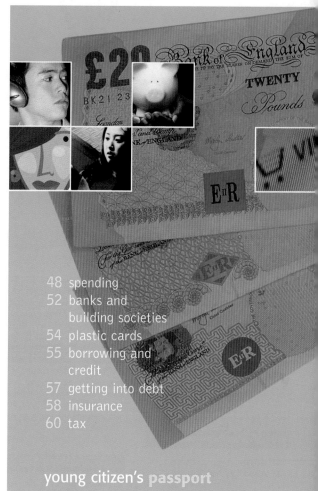

young citizen's passport

INDIVIDUALS
ENGAGING IN
SOCIETY

Citizenship Foundation

It's a contract

When you buy something from a shop or pay for a service (like a train fare or haircut) you are making an agreement, known in law as a *contract*.

The contract means that, in return for the money that you pay, the goods you buy should do everything you can reasonably expect and, in particular, all that the seller and manufacturer claim.

Once a contract has been agreed, neither side can change it on their own. Some shops allow customers to opt out of their contract by agreeing to exchange unwanted items or by providing a refund, as long as goods are returned in mint condition with the receipt. Shops don't have to do this by law, unless it was promised as part of the contract.

But what about your rights if the goods you have bought are faulty?

The Sale of Goods Act

The law applying to most everyday purchases is the *Sale of Goods Act 1979*. This was updated in 2003 to provide new protection for consumers. It says that when you buy goods from a shop or trader, they must …

…be of satisfactory quality

This means that they must be free from faults and not scratched or damaged, and equally applies to goods bought in a sale. However, this rule does not apply if the fault was pointed out by the sales assistant or if you inspected the item and had a good opportunity to discover the fault.

Second-hand goods bought from a shop or trader must also be of satisfactory quality. This protection does not apply if you bought the goods privately (e.g. through a 'small ad') – when the buyer is responsible for deciding the quality of what she or he wants to buy.

…match the description

The goods must be the same as the description on the packaging, or advertisement or given by the assistant at the time of sale. A bracelet marked solid silver, must be just that.

This rule also applies to second-hand goods, including those sold privately.

…be fit for all their intended purposes

This means that they must do what the seller, packaging or advertisements claim. A watch sold as waterproof should not stop if you forget to take it off in the shower.

GETTING IT RIGHT

If you're buying something expensive, and want to do some research beforehand, *Which?* magazine, available in most libraries and on the Internet, gives a guide to the price and performance of many products. You can also go to a shop and ask just to see an item, without buying it. If you decide to make a purchase, keep the receipt in case you have a complaint.

Services too

Dry cleaners, shoe repairers, hairdressers, travel agents and many others provide a service - and you are protected by law if that service is inadequate.

Under the *Supply of Goods and Services Act 1982*, a service must be provided...

- **with reasonable care and skill;**
- **within a reasonable time; and**
- **for a reasonable charge.**

Problems? Problems are less likely to occur if certain things are agreed before the work is started. How much will it cost? How long will it take? What happens if the work can't be finished? Try to sort these out first.

Handle your complaint just as you would were it for faulty goods. Don't be afraid to seek advice. Help is available from your local Citizens Advice Bureau or consumer advice centre.

Some trades, such as travel agents, garages, dry cleaners, shoe sellers etc have their own associations laying down a code of practice or standards. These have no legal standing, but the associations can put pressure on their members to treat customers' complaints in a reasonable way. It may be worth a try, and your local library can give you the address to contact.

spending

PUT DOWNS

Some businesses will do as much as they can to help you with a problem over something you have bought; others may claim that there is nothing they can do. Don't give up if the shop tries to get out of its legal obligations...

...we'll send it back to the workshop

Only if you want them to. If you act reasonably quickly you can choose whether to ask for a full or partial refund, compensation or to have the goods repaired or replaced (if that is a practical option). If the goods have developed a fault in the first six months it is assumed they were faulty when you bought them (unless the shop can prove otherwise).

... you'll have to take it up with the manufacturer

Wrong. You bought the goods from the shop and your contract was with them, not with a manufacturer on the other side of the world. If the goods genuinely don't work, the shop has not kept its side of the contract and you have a right to your money back. Shops normally have to accept responsibility to you for the manufacturer's claims.

...we'll give you a credit note

No. If the goods are faulty, you're entitled to your money back. You don't have to accept a credit note if you don't want to. If you do accept a credit note, check where and when you can use it – some credit notes must be used within a fixed time and only in exchange for certain goods or services.

...sorry, it's out of guarantee

This can be tricky. A major problem with an expensive computer three months after the guarantee has run out means a large repair bill. Raise it with the dealer and ask to talk to the manager. Produce the documentation and use the manufacturer's literature (which probably stresses reliability and quality) to point out that it is not reasonable to expect a failure after such a short period. There's no hard and fast law about what is reasonable in terms of a product failure. It depends on the circumstances.

...we don't give refunds on sale goods

Wrong. Unless the fault was pointed out to you or was something you should have seen when you bought them, goods bought in sales carry all the protection of the *Sale of Goods Act 1979*.

...we'll give you a replacement

Only if that's what you want. However, if by now the fault has led you to decide that you don't really want the product after all, you are entitled to your money back - not a replacement. It's up to you to choose what to do.

50

The small claims court

If you cannot get any satisfaction over a problem with faulty goods or poor service, you can write to the person concerned warning them that you will try to recover the money they owe you by taking your case to the small claims court (strictly known as the small claims procedure). This is an informal way of settling disputes, at a fraction of the normal cost, in which a judge hears your case without the expense of lawyers. Cases usually involve claims of less than £5,000 and can be brought only by someone of 18 or over. You can get more details from your local county court (under Courts in the phone book), the Citizens Advice Bureau or a consumer advice centre, see **contacts**.

Finding it's wrong

If you are not satisfied with something that you have bought....

> Stop using it straightaway and take it back, with the receipt and guarantee (if you have one), to the shop where you bought it. It strengthens your case if you can do this as soon as possible. Your contract was with the shop, not the manufacturer, so it is the shop's responsibility to deal with your complaint. Even if you have lost the receipt, the contract still exists.

> Before you take the goods back, decide what you are going to say and what you would like the shop to do. Do you want your money back, or will you accept a repair or a replacement item?

> Think about your legal position. A faulty stop button on a personal stereo means that it is not of satisfactory quality. Don't be afraid to use the law when making your case.

> If the shop assistant doesn't help, ask for someone more senior.

> If you bought the goods by mail order or from a shop some distance away, it's easier to telephone or write. Keep a copy of all letters, send a photocopy of your receipt (keep the original), and if you talk on the phone get the name of the person you spoke to. Make a brief note of the conversation.

Buying over the phone or on the Internet

The same rules apply as when you buy from a shop but the trader must give you some basic information like the name and address of the person you are dealing with and, in most cases, you should be given the chance to cancel your order within seven days.

You can get more details from the Office of Fair Trading or a Citizens Advice Bureau; see **contacts**.

A regular bank account is normally only available if you are 18 or over (or are 16 or 17 with a steady income or there is an adult who will act as your guarantor). A basic or starter account may be available from 16.

WHY HAVE AN ACCOUNT?

- many employers insist on paying salary or wages directly into an account;
- an account is needed for a student loan;
- the money can earn interest;
- regular accounts come with a cheque book and plastic card to pay for things;
- you can pay cheques other people give you into an account;

CHOOSING A BANK OR BUILDING SOCIETY

You will probably want to know:
- whether it has a branch near you and offers on-line banking;
- whether there are convenient cash points;
- the services offered and the charges;
- the level of interest paid on the money you have in the account. There will be leaflets on this, or you can ask a member of staff; and,
- its special offers for young people. But don't be persuaded by offers of free gifts if the services and charges are unattractive compared with other banks or building societies.

What types of accounts are there?

The two main types are current accounts and savings accounts.

Current accounts

A current account is the normal account for day-to-day transactions. You pay in the money you receive, such as your wages, salary or student loan.

If you are 18 or over, you can usually get a chequebook and a cheque guarantee card so that you can pay for things by giving a signed cheque. You may also be given one or more plastic cards. These are described on page 54.

You'll receive a regular bank statement – probably once a month – to show how much has been paid in, how much you have withdrawn and your balance.

Using a cheque book and guarantee card

A chequebook contains a number of cheques with your name on. The person you give a cheque to pays it into their bank account, and after a few days the money is taken (debited) from your account and added (credited) to the other person's account.

If you haven't got enough money in your current account to cover the value of the cheque you have written the bank may refuse to honour your cheque and it will bounce.

You may also be issued with a cheque guarantee card. This enables you to pay for things more easily, as it guarantees that the bank will honour your cheque up to the amount stated

on the card – usually £50 or £100. If there isn't enough money in your account to cover the value of the cheques you have written with your cheque guarantee card, you'll go overdrawn and may have to pay bank charges and interest. Strictly speaking it is an offence to write a cheque when you know there is not enough money in your account to cover it, unless you already have the permission of your bank to do so; see page 55.

What do I do if someone gives me a cheque? When someone pays you by cheque, look to see that is correctly written out, that it is for the right amount, that it has been signed, and that it is not "post-dated" (one with a future date on).

As soon as possible pay the cheque into your current account using a paying in slip. Cheques that are more than six months old may not be accepted.

Savings accounts A savings account provides a higher rate of interest. Most do not come with a chequebook or plastic card, and some have restrictions on when you can withdraw your money. However, you will still be able to withdraw money if you really have to, but will probably lose some of the extra interest.

If you keep money in your savings account at the same time as being overdrawn on your current account or having a loan, you may find the interest you pay on your overdraft or loan is higher than the interest you earn on your savings account - so you will be worse off.

What about tax on the interest I earn? Interest earned on bank and building society accounts is usually paid after tax has been deducted from it. Unless you have a high income, that is normally the end of the matter, and there is no more tax to pay; see **tax** page 60. If you are not a taxpayer - because your earnings are not high enough - you can either get the tax back by contacting a tax office or you can choose to have the interest paid to you without deduction of the tax. Your bank or building society will have the forms for you to complete that allow them to do this.

plastic cards

If you buy something with a credit card, that costs £100 or more, and it turns out to be faulty or not what you paid for, you can make a claim against the credit card company as well as the person who sold you the goods. This does not apply to payments made with a debit or charge card.

| What about plastic cards? | Plastic cards can be extremely useful. But they can cause difficulties if you are not careful how you use them. You |

usually have to be 18 to get one. There are many types of card with different functions:

- **Cheque guarantee card** - See page 52. This should not be kept with your chequebook.
- **Cash card** - This enables you to get cash from cash machines. You will be given a confidential personal identity number - PIN - to use with your card. It is essential that no one else knows your PIN. Never keep a record of it with your card. If you do, anyone stealing it can immediately get at your cash.
- **Debit card e.g. Switch** - This card allows you to buy things without writing a cheque or using cash. You can also use it to pay for goods over the telephone or on the Internet. Your account is automatically debited with the amount you have spent. You can only go overdrawn with a debit card, if you have the bank's agreement.

- **Credit card e.g. Mastercard and Visa** - Like a debit card, holding a credit card allows people to purchase goods and services from a huge range of shops and other suppliers, including over the telephone or on the Internet. A credit card, however, allows the shop to be paid now but the customer does not receive the bill until later.
  The firm issuing the credit card is, in

If you lose a card or your chequebook, notify the card company or bank immediately. They can often be contacted 24 hours a day. If your card is lost or stolen and used by someone else before you have reported the loss you may have to pay the first £50 of any debts incurred.

effect, lending the customer the money to buy things. The bank will check out their customers' credit worthiness. They may charge a yearly fee for the card. When a credit card account is opened a spending limit is set. If this is broken, the card may be cancelled.

Each month a statement is sent to the customer, showing what has been spent using the card, how much is owed, and what minimum payment must be made. Cardholders who do not pay off their bill in full are charged a high rate of interest.

Customers can compare the costs of different cards by looking at the Annual Percentage Rate (APR). The APR is the rate of interest charged by the firm issuing the credit card. All organisations issuing cards have to quote their APR, which shows the total cost of the credit. A credit card with a high APR costs more than one with a low APR.

- **Store card** - These are credit cards issued by stores, for example department stores or sports shops. You open an account with the store that in effect lends you money to buy their goods or services.

They will send you a regular statement showing how much you have spent, and how much you owe them. With some cards, you have to pay off the full amount each month. With others, you may be able to pay a fixed minimum amount each time; the rest will be carried forward and appear on your next statement.

You will have to pay interest on the amount you haven't paid off. These interest charges can be high. You can check the APR and compare it with your credit card.

borrowing and credit

Borrowing from a bank or building society A bank or building society lends money either through allowing an overdraft or by making a loan.

Overdrafts A person becomes overdrawn when they spend more money than they have in their bank account. The most expensive overdraft is an unauthorised one - which is run up without the agreement of the bank. Interest is paid on the amount overdrawn, and charges are added on top.

If you ever find yourself in this situation, it is important to get in touch with the bank soon as you can.

If you need to go overdrawn, you can usually arrange with your bank an authorised overdraft, up to an agreed amount. Interest may be charged. Students may be offered interest free overdrafts.

borrowing and credit

LOANS

A loan is an arrangement with your bank - or other financial institution - under which you are lent a specific amount of money. You enter into a contract for the loan. This will be for a set period, with an agreed rate of interest and time over which you have to repay the full amount. If you are under 18 it is very unlikely that you will be able to get a bank loan, as contracts with "minors" are not usually binding so the bank will be taking too big a risk.

A loan is usually a better way of borrowing money than running up large debts on a credit card, but it is important to check that the repayment terms are affordable.

Buying goods by instalments - credit or hire purchase

You can often buy more expensive goods (cars, hi-fi systems, TVs) by instalment - that is, by paying only part of the price at the time of purchase, and paying the rest later. This is known as buying on credit or on tick. Sometimes credit is available interest free, but credit is normally an expensive way of paying for things. It is always a good idea to check the charges (the APR) that are being made .

Hire purchase is a special form of buying on credit. Technically the shop sells the goods to a finance company and you pay to "hire" them over an agreed period. When you have paid off what you owe you make a small final payment to purchase the goods (hence "hire purchase"). Only then do you become the owner.

Second thoughts If you signed a credit deal at home (or away from the shop or business premises) you have a right to cancel if you act quickly. You will be sent a second copy of the agreement that will tell you how to cancel if you want to. If you signed the agreement on business premises then it's much harder to cancel unless the form has to be sent away to the credit company for its signature. Then you can withdraw as long as you tell them before they have signed up.

use the law with care try talking first

getting into debt

People get into debt for all sorts of reasons, often through no fault of their own. They may find they owe money to several different people and are tempted to borrow more to pay off some of these debts. This often becomes even more expensive.

You know it's getting serious when you start getting badgered to make repayments by the people you owe money to - your "creditors" - and you can't meet all the demands.

What to do

- **Don't ignore the problem:** it won't go away and will get worse the longer you leave it. You can get help and, in most cases, you can take control.

- **Draw up a budget:** list all the money you owe and the people to whom it is owed; what your income and reasonable living expenses are; and see how much you can afford to pay back.

- **List your debts in their order of priority:** at the top are those where non payment can have really serious consequences - like losing your flat or home; having the electricity or gas cut off, or where non payment is a criminal offence (like council tax and your TV licence). You should aim to pay these off first and then work out what's left over for the others, treating them equally.

- **Contact all your creditors:** go and see them or write or phone; explain the position and show them your budget. Discuss with them what you can reasonably pay. Usually they will be prepared to negotiate an agreement with you as this improves their chances of getting paid. You may be able to agree to pay by instalments or, for a period of time, just to pay off the interest on your loan.

- **Don't borrow more without getting advice:** there are lots of people prepared to lend you more to pay off earlier debts. They are sometimes called loan-sharks. They will probably charge very high rates of interest making it even more difficult for you to get out of debt. They won't be nearly as easy to deal with if you can't keep up your repayments

HELP

You can get help and advice from experts. Try the National Debtline or a Citizens Advice Bureau. See contacts.

Insurance is a way of protecting yourself and your property from an unexpected loss or mishap. You can insure yourself against almost anything - losing your possessions in a fire, having them stolen or damaged, or having to face unexpected medical bills on holiday abroad. If you drive a car or motorcycle, you must be insured by law, see Travel and transport, page 97 .

In return for a premium - an agreed amount of money you pay each month or year - an insurance company will, if the worst does happen, pay you compensation for the losses or damage that you insured against.

Buying insurance

There are two ways of obtaining insurance. You can either deal directly with the company, or go to a broker. Most large insurance companies have offices in the major towns and cities. Their numbers are in the Yellow Pages or local phone book. You can often deal directly with them and arrange your insurance cover by phone.

Insurance brokers are agents who can help you choose an insurer and arrange the policy for you. They don't usually charge you for this, but instead make their money from the insurance company that you have decided to use.

All the information you give should be as accurate as possible. Questions must be answered truthfully, and any other information that could be relevant should also be given. If it's not, the insurance policy will be invalid.

Keep a copy of any form that you complete, and when you renew your insurance (usually done each year) don't forget to tell the insurance company about anything that has changed that might affect your insurance position.

THE WORDS THEY USE:

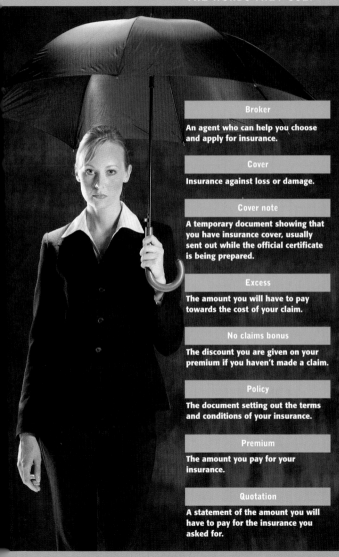

Broker
An agent who can help you choose and apply for insurance.

Cover
Insurance against loss or damage.

Cover note
A temporary document showing that you have insurance cover, usually sent out while the official certificate is being prepared.

Excess
The amount you will have to pay towards the cost of your claim.

No claims bonus
The discount you are given on your premium if you haven't made a claim.

Policy
The document setting out the terms and conditions of your insurance.

Premium
The amount you pay for your insurance.

Quotation
A statement of the amount you will have to pay for the insurance you asked for.

tax

Income Tax

Money paid in income tax is used to pay for services provided by the state - such as health, education, defence etc. Everyone who earns or receives income over a certain amount in a year pays income tax and, generally speaking, the more you earn, the more you pay. As well as earnings from full and part-time work, tips and bonuses, tax is also paid on interest from savings with banks, building societies and some National Savings accounts, on Income Support and on profits from a business and dividends from shares.

PAYE Your employer will usually take the tax from your earnings each time you are paid and pass the money on to the tax authorities, called the Inland Revenue. Everyone is entitled to receive a certain amount of money on which they pay no tax at all. This is called a personal allowance, which, for a single person in 2003/2004, is £4,615. Income tax is paid only when your income rises above this. There are other allowances which may be available, e.g. for the cost of tools or special clothing if they are not provided by your employer. If you are on a training programme, your grant in most cases is not taxable.

Part-time workers should not have tax deducted from their pay, unless their income is above £89 a week. If you are a student with a holiday job, ask your employer for a form P38(S) if you think your total taxable income for the year (including earnings and income support), will be less than the basic personal allowance, i.e. £4,615. Fill in the form, return it to your employer, and you should then be paid without tax being deducted.

If you have been working and paying tax, but believe your total income for the year will be less than £4,615 ask for form P50 from your local tax office, and return it completed with your P45 from your employer. The Inland Revenue publishes free booklets on tax, obtainable from your library or nearest tax office (under Inland Revenue in the phone book). The Taxpayer's Charter outlines the service you are entitled to expect from staff at the Inland Revenue. Failure to complete your tax forms correctly can mean extra interest payments and even fines. The Inland Revenue runs a telephone helpline, giving information and advice on tax, see **contacts**.

Tax credits Working Tax Credits and Child Tax Credits are available to those on low incomes to top up earnings.

BENEFITS

You may be entitled to Income Support, Jobseeker's Allowance, Maternity Allowance, a disability allowance or other social security benefits. Benefit rates normally change once a year, in April. Leaflets explaining this are available from Social Security and Jobcentre Plus offices, and sometimes local libraries and post offices. A freephone benefits information and advice line for disabled people and their carers is available on 0800 88 22 00.

family

young citizen's passport

INDIVIDUALS
ENGAGING IN
SOCIETY

Citizenship Foundation

Within six weeks of birth, the birth and name of a child must be registered with the District Registrar of Births, Marriages and Deaths. The birth may be registered either in the district in which it took place or elsewhere.

The birth can be registered by either parent if they are married, but only by the mother if they are not. If unmarried parents want both their names to appear on their child's birth certificate, then they must both be present when the child is registered. Names can also be registered later.

Changing your name

Under 18 A child's name can be changed with the agreement of both parents, unless the child is in care or a ward of court. In this case the child's name cannot be changed without the agreement of the court or everyone with responsibility for the child. The child can also object by applying to court.

If a parent wants to change their child's name, but the other parent or the child objects - then the parent or the child can apply for a court order to prevent this. Courts are very reluctant to agree to change a child's name against their wish because of the importance of a name to a child's sense of identity.

If you wish to change your name you will need your parents' agreement or a court order. If you are over 16 you can change your name by deed poll and register it at court. If your parents object, you may need a court order to override their objection.

Over 18 You can call yourself what you like and, if you want to change your name, you can just go ahead and do it. If you are married, you will usually need the agreement of your spouse. But you can't change your name to mislead or defraud someone.

Although you are free to be known by whatever name you wish, it can be difficult to prove your identity if the name you use is not the same as the one on your birth certificate. The best way to confirm your new name is by a change of name deed poll, which is a statement announcing your new name, witnessed by a solicitor. Your local Citizens Advice Bureau or a solicitor can give you more information on this.

If you marry

Women have the right to change their surname when they marry - but they don't have to. A woman can keep her own family name, or make a new one by joining her name with that of her husband. A new surname becomes official by signing the marriage register or a deed poll.

A man can change his name to that of his wife upon marriage with her consent and by using a deed poll.

CITIZENSHIP

Most of our legal rights and responsibilities arise just because we are living, working, studying etc. in a particular place - in our case, Britain. This is citizenship in its widest sense.

Sometimes, however, people need to know which country they are legally connected to (or what their nationality is). Countries can base their rules on a number of questions, such as where the person was born, how long they have lived in the country and where their parents were born or live.

In brief Anyone born in the United Kingdom before 1 January 1983 is automatically a British citizen. If you were born in the UK on or after this date, you are a British citizen by birth if either of your parents are British citizens or they are entitled to live here permanently. If your parents are not married, only your mother's position counts.

Becoming a British citizen by naturalisation or registration depends on a number of different factors, such as if you marry a British citizen, how long you have lived here, if you are permanently settled here (or intend to remain here permanently) and if you are of 'good character'.

This is a complicated process and you will need specialist advice. Your local Citizens Advice Bureau can help you find this.

parents

How the law works

There are no laws that list the exact rights and duties of parents. It is impossible to write down everything a parent should do for a child.

Instead, the law states that all married parents and unmarried mothers automatically have parental responsibility for their children. An unmarried father does not have automatic parental responsibility for his child. He can obtain parental responsibility by signing the birth register jointly with the mother, by agreement with her, by marrying her, or by being granted parental responsibility by the courts.

Parental responsibility This means having the responsibility and authority to care for the child's physical, moral, and emotional needs.

When a child or young person is taken into care, parental responsibility is given to the local authority, although parents do keep certain rights and responsibilities.

The law puts the interest of the child first. The powers that parents have to control their children are for the benefit of the child, not the parent. Those who deal with children in a legal setting, such as social workers, doctors and lawyers, must take careful note of what a child says, particularly when the child is able to understand all the issues involved. Parental responsibility ends when the child reaches 18. As a very experienced judge once said; "in law, parents begin with a right of control, but by the time the child is 18 they can do no more than advise."

Providing a home

Parents have a duty to look after and care for their children until they are 18. However, once someone reaches the age of 16 they can normally leave home without their parent's permission. The police and other authorities are unlikely to stop anyone leaving home, even against their parent's wishes, unless they are under 16, in some kind of danger, or are unable to look after themselves. See **home**, page 73.

Discipline

Parents have the right and duty to discipline their child - and this can include smacking. But corporal punishment must be "moderate and reasonable". If it is too harsh the parents risk prosecution or having their child's name put on the child protection register or the child being taken into care. In several other European countries, it is illegal for a parent to strike a child and this is being considered in parts of Britain.

Education

Parents have a duty to make sure that their child has a suitable full-time education, between the ages of 5-16. See **education**, page 24.

BABY-SITTING

Religion

Parents can decide the religion (if any) in which their child will be brought up. If they can't agree between themselves, they can go to court, where a judge will decide what is in the best interests of the child.

A court will listen to the views the child concerned and these will be respected if the child clearly understands what is involved.

Medical treatment

In practice young people, aged 16 and over, can almost always agree to their own medical treatment without referring to their parents. Before treating a young person under 16, however, a doctor will normally try to obtain the parent's permission unless it is an emergency or the young person is clearly able to understand what the treatment involves.

There is no law giving the minimum age for a baby-sitter, nor one stating how old a child must be before it can be left alone. Parents must take all the circumstances into account. For example, the age of the baby sitter, the availability of the parent(s) or the health of the children being looked after, count as relevant factors.

Parents have a legal duty to care for their children; some of that responsibility is temporarily passed on to a baby-sitter when the children are in their care. This means that parents must choose a baby-sitter who is able to look after their children properly. If a serious accident occurs while they are out, the parents may have to convince a court that they had done all that they could to make sure their child was being looked after properly. A baby-sitter under 16 will probably be thought too young to deal with an emergency.

adoption

Anyone who is under 18, and has never been married, can be adopted.

A couple or an individual wishing to adopt a child must usually be at least 21. If a married couple wish to adopt, and one partner is the father or mother of the child, they need only be 18.

When children are adopted, they are treated in law almost as if they had been born to the couple or person who adopted them. Parents who adopt children are advised to be open about their child's birth family from the start.

At 18, people who have been adopted have the right to see a copy of their original birth records, and can get more information from the agency that arranged their adoption. An interview with a counsellor to prepare them for this is available.

Further help for adopted people and their birth relatives who wish to get in touch is available through the Adoption Contact Register and NORCAP. See life, page 6, and contacts.

An increasing number of couples live together, sometimes with the thought of getting married later on, and sometimes not. Although this is a matter of personal choice, the law treats married and unmarried couples very differently.

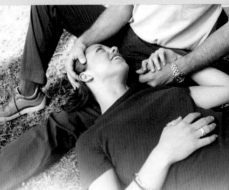

Money and finance

A couple who live together without getting married are under no duty to look after one another, or to provide each other with financial support, unless it is something they have specifically agreed to do.

When children are involved, both parents, whether married or unmarried, have a legal responsibility to look after them and provide for them until they reach the age of 16, or up to 19 if they remain in full-time education.

If a married person dies without making a will, their partner is entitled to all or most of their possessions. But if they were not married, it can be very difficult for the partner to obtain any of the deceased's possessions.

Children

Parents who are married share parental responsibility for their children. This means that both can make decisions about their children's upbringing. Unmarried fathers have this right if the couple have signed a parental responsibility agreement, or if the father has made a successful application to court for parental responsibility.

Home

A married couple have equal rights to occupy their home, whether they rent or own it. This continues even if their marriage fails, unless the court orders otherwise.

Unmarried couples do not have this right. If the home is in just one person's name, the non-owner may not have any right to occupy the property. However, non-owners can obtain rights over the house if they make mortgage payments or improvements to the structure of the property. Couples can avoid difficulties caused by this by using a solicitor to write a formal contract setting out what would happen to their house and contents etc. should the relationship come to an end.

Breaking up Unlike a married couple, people who live together can end their relationship anytime they choose, without having to go to court.

Getting married

Legally, no one can be forced to marry against their wishes, and each partner must be 16 or over and unmarried. A person who wants to marry, but is under 18, needs their parents' written consent. It's a criminal offence if a couple get married without this, but the marriage is still valid. However marriages involving someone aged 15 or under, or members of the same sex (even after a sex change operation), are not recognised in law.

Almost anyone can be married in an Anglican church (unless they are divorced and their former partner is still alive). They need not be a churchgoer, but must satisfy the legal requirements and qualify as a resident of the parish. Members of other faiths must, before the religious ceremony, obtain a civil certificate or licence from the senior registrar in the district where they live.

Under the *Marriage Acts*, couples can choose to marry in any registry office in England and Wales or in other places that have been registered (such as a hotel or stately home).

Being married to more than one person at the same time - called bigamy - is normally a crime. But the marriages are recognised in England and Wales if they took place in a country that allows marriages of this kind, and if each partner was legally free to marry in that way.

Engagement

Until 1970 an engagement was seen as a legal contract. If someone breaks off their engagement today there is usually not even a duty to return the engagement ring. The ring is seen as a gift, and may be kept, unless it was originally agreed to return it if the marriage did not take place.

VIOLENCE

A court can make an order, called an injunction, to protect a victim of domestic violence and can order one partner to leave the home for the other's protection - even if they are married. It is important for anyone in this situation to get advice from a solicitor as soon as possible.

divorce

A couple who no longer wish to live together, can either end their marriage by divorce, or separate, keeping the marriage legally alive. A separation may simply mean living apart, or it can be made more formal through a court order.

When one or both partners decide to divorce, an application is made to the local county court or, in London, the Divorce Registry. It is usually made through a solicitor, but can be done by one of the partners alone (but not until at least one year after the date of marriage).

If both partners can agree over their finances and together make satisfactory plans for the care of their children, it will probably not be necessary for either to appear in court. Nor will there be any publicity in the papers. There are thousands of divorces each year, and the press cannot report the case unless the divorce is contested or reporting restrictions are lifted.

When the Judge is satisfied that the appropriate arrangements have been made, that all the information is correct and that the marriage has broken down and cannot be saved, he or she will grant a decree nisi - the first stage in obtaining the divorce. Six weeks later, the person seeking the divorce can apply for a decree absolute. When this is granted, the marriage comes to an end.

Grounds for divorce

A person who applies for a divorce must prove to the court that their marriage has irretrievably broken down and that one of the following five things has happened....

I think you are seeing someone else

1. the other partner has committed adultery, ie had sexual intercourse with another man or woman and it is intolerable to live together;

2. the other partner has behaved unreasonably. This covers many things, including assault, refusing to have children, being excessively dirty or anti-social;

3. they have lived apart for two years, and they both want a divorce;

4. they have lived apart for five years and only one partner wants a

5. divorce; or one partner has deserted the other for at least two years immediately before the application.

Children

Parents going through a divorce are encouraged to reach an agreement between themselves over where their children will live and how often they will see each parent. But the judge will accept these arrangements only if satisfied that they are in the best interests of the child. If the child is felt to be old enough to have a view of their own, the judge will talk to them in private.

Parents who cannot agree over this are often advised not to go straight to court (expensive and stressful for all concerned), but to use independent counsellors to help them sort out their problems. A court will, however, have to approve the final arrangements over children and money. It's usually felt to be in the children's interest to keep in touch with their family, so a judge will rarely stop a parent from seeing a child.

After the divorce, both parents normally keep parental responsibility for their child, and both should consult each other over decisions that affect their child's life, such as education, medical treatment, and religious upbringing.

Step-parents

Step-parents do not have parental responsibility for their stepchildren, but the courts can require them to support a step-child. With their new partner, the step-parent may help with day-to-day things affecting the child, but major decisions should be taken by the child's birth mother and father - or only the mother, if they were not married (unless the father has parental responsibility). To change this, a step-parent may apply for parental responsibility or, together with the birthparent, to adopt the child. See **contacts** for organisations able to give more information about this. If their relationship with the natural parent breaks down, the step-parent will have no rights over the child.

divorce

Grandparents

When a marriage ends, it may mean that a child is prevented from seeing other family members, such as grandparents, adding to the child's loss. In this situation, grandparents can apply to a court for permission to carry on seeing the child or to have the child stay with them - although this is more difficult to obtain than for parents.

Family disputes

Sometimes parents become involved in legal disputes which directly affect their children - especially if they are getting divorced and cannot agree who the children should live with. In really important cases a young person who shows enough understanding of the issues, can act on their own initiative to instruct a solicitor and even make an application to the Court. It is usually much better if their views can be reflected through a counsellor or mediator as the whole process can be very stressful and damaging to relationships with parents or other family members. It is important to get specialist advice, see **contacts**.

home

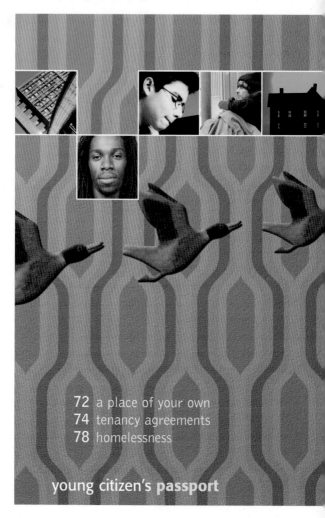

young citizen's passport

INDIVIDUALS ENGAGING IN SOCIETY

Citizenship Foundation

a place of your own

Where do I look?

Advertisements for accommodation are found in local newspapers, supermarkets and the student union, if you are at college. The local council housing department can tell you whether you are likely to qualify for council housing, and can also give you details of local housing associations.

You can also try estate agents and accommodation agencies. These agencies are not allowed, by law, to charge you for information about housing or lists of vacancies. Don't agree to pay them a fee. Normally they are paid for their services by the landlord. If you are asked for money and have any doubts, check first with the local Citizens Advice Bureau or Shelterline, see **contacts**. Don't be rushed. It's a good idea to get someone to look at the place with you.

You can't buy or rent a house or get a mortgage if you are under 18.

What's the rent?

What does it include - council tax, electricity etc? How often is it paid, and who is it paid to? Is any rent payable in advance? Rent paid in advance will be lost if you leave without giving the right amount of notice.

Your rent is fixed at whatever rate you agreed with your landlord. If you think the rent demanded is too high you can ask the local rent assessment committee to decide what is reasonable for the property (ring your local council, or see under 'rent officer' in the phone book). If you are an assured shorthold tenant (most are), you must do this within the first six months of the tenancy. There is no charge for this, but the committee can assess your rent only if there are enough similar flats or houses being let in the area.

The rate fixed by the rent assessment committee applies for at least 12 months from the date the rent was fixed, and a tenant can make only one application to the

HOUSING BENEFIT

If you are on a training programme, Income Support or a low wage, you may qualify for Housing Benefit from your local council. Your local housing advice centre or Citizens Advice Bureau can help you work out what you're entitled to. Housing Benefit is not available to full-time students, unless they have children or have a disability.

Discrimination

A landlord must not discriminate against a would-be tenant on grounds of race or sex, unless the property is being shared with others, and the landlord (or close relatives) live at the property. It is also against the law for someone who sells or lets property to discriminate against a disabled person. Landlords and members of their immediate family who let out rooms to less than seven people in their own homes are not affected.

use the law with care **try talking first**

committee. It's a good idea to take advice before you do this, as your landlord may try to evict you. Sometimes the committee can put the rent up as well as down.

Do I pay a deposit? This is an amount (often equal to a month's rent) paid to the landlord, or the agent, at the start of the tenancy. Always ask for a receipt when you hand over your deposit.

If you cause damage or leave bills or rent unpaid, the landlord can take what you owe from your deposit. Try to agree any deductions with the landlord before you leave, otherwise you may find you've lost more of your deposit than you should.

Is there a service charge? This is money paid to look after the building and clean those parts that are shared, such as the stairs and corridors in a block of flats. Check what is covered by this figure and decide whether it seems reasonable. If you rent your home from a private landlord or a housing association and pay a variable service charge as well as rent, you have the right to ask the landlord exactly how the service charge is calculated.

Do I need references? If so, choose people who have known you for a reasonable length of time, but preferably not a close relative. It is important to ask the person concerned first.

How safe? Check the fire escape, plumbing, electrical fittings, and heating appliances. Landlords must, by law, have all gas appliances checked each year and must get a certificate of safety that you are entitled to see.

Leaving home

Young people under 18 are still, in law, in the "custody and care" of their parents, which means that, strictly speaking, they need their parent's permission to leave home. But, in reality, courts are unlikely to order anyone aged 16 or 17 to return home who leaves home against their parents' wishes, unless they appear to be in some kind of danger or unable to look after themselves. See also **family**, page 64.

If you are 16 or 17 and homeless, or feel that you can no longer live at home because you are being hurt, or because life at home is so bad, you can get help from social services. Under the *Children Act 1989*, local authorities must provide accommodation for 16 and 17 year olds who are in need or whose welfare would be endangered if accommodation were not provided. However, some local authorities find it difficult to get hold of suitable accommodation for young people, and Income Support is not available to all 16 or 17 year olds. Therefore, if you can, get advice from a housing advice centre, Citizens Advice Bureau, or your local council before you do anything.

In care If you are leaving care, your local social services have a legal duty to provide help and advice.

tenancy agreements

When you rent a flat or house, you normally sign an agreement with the landlord or their agent. This is known in law as a tenancy agreement, sometimes called a lease.

It should contain all the conditions agreed between you and the landlord, along with a list (called an inventory) of the furniture and other equipment that comes with the property. Make sure everything is included, and make a note of anything that's damaged when you take up the property.

Read all documents carefully. Don't be afraid to seek advice from the Citizens Advice Bureau, a housing advice centre, or a solicitor if parts are not clear, or if they contain conditions which you didn't expect. Don't sign until you fully understand the agreement and are prepared to accept what it says.

Normally you and the landlord will each sign, exchange and keep a copy of the tenancy agreement. Look after this. If there's any kind of problem while you're in the property, you'll need it to check your rights and duties.

| Assured shorthold tenancy | This is the name given to the kind of tenancy that you will probably have if you rent a house or a flat. |

In fact, if your tenancy agreement was made on or after 28 February 1997, it must be of this type, unless you have some kind of written statement from the landlord saying it is not.

Your tenancy agreement will probably work like this....

- You are "assured" of the right to stay as a tenant for the period stated in the agreement, unless you break the agreement in some way, in which case the landlord can apply to a court to get you to leave earlier. Assured shorthold tenancies used to be for a period of at least six months. This minimum period no longer applies.
- You can't leave before the end of this time, without being required to pay the balance of the rent, unless your tenancy agreement has a "break clause" allowing you to leave early by serving an agreed period of notice, such as one month. You can ask for this to be included in your agreement.
- You have a right to receive from your landlord a written statement of the terms of your tenancy. This includes the date that the tenancy began, the date that it ends, the amount of rent payable, and the date that it is due. The landlord can be prosecuted and fined if this information is not provided within 28 days of your request.
- The landlord must give you at

use the law with care try talking first

least two months' notice to leave. With a six-month tenancy this will normally be at the end of the fourth month.

- If the landlord delays this and does not serve notice until the fifth or sixth month, or even later, you have the right (assuming you continue to pay the rent), to stay in the property for a further two months.

- If you stay on without the landlord's permission after the two months' notice has expired, the landlord is entitled to apply to a court for an order to have you evicted. This will almost certainly be granted, and you will then be expected to pay the costs of the court order as well as the rent for the extra time in the property. It is illegal for a landlord to evict you without a court order (see eviction, page 76).

- If you take on an assured shorthold tenancy you are legally responsible for the rent up to the end of the agreed period. If you are sharing the flat or house with someone and they leave, then their share of the rent must still be paid until a replacement is found.

Lodging and hostels

You do not have the same rights if you are in lodgings or if your landlord lives with you in the same house and shares the basic services with you. Your landlady or landlord only needs to give you "reasonable notice" (this can be seven days), and does not need to apply to a court to have you evicted.

If you are in hostel accommodation with a local council or housing association, they will not generally need a court order to evict you. They can give you notice at any time, as long as they keep to the terms of the tenancy agreement.

Council tenants

You have certain rights as a council tenant, which include staying in your house for as long as you want (assuming you pay your rent and do what your tenancy agreement says), taking in lodgers, and being consulted about the running of the estate. The council has a right to take action against tenants who cause a nuisance to others on the estate. In serious cases this has led to tenants losing their homes.

Who is responsible?

Repairs and maintenance

If your tenancy agreement is for less than seven years, as it almost certainly will be, your landlord is responsible by law for looking after the structure of the building, including outside fittings (such as gutters) and essential services (heating appliances - not cookers - sinks, baths and toilets and the water, gas and electricity supplies). Responsibility for other repairs depends on what is said in the tenancy agreement. Tenants are normally responsible for repairs for damage that they cause, but not for fair "wear and tear".

Getting them done

Tell the landlord when the repairs need doing - and keep paying the rent. If the landlord does nothing and the problem concerns serious questions of health and safety, you can get in touch with the local environmental health office. They have the powers to get something done, and can make the landlord carry out the necessary work. Their number is in the phone book under the name of your local council.

If the problem is not serious, or the local council won't take action, check again that responsibility for the work lies with your landlord. If it does, write to the landlord explaining you intend to undertake the work yourself and send at least three estimates of the cost. Give your landlord at least two weeks to consider these. If, at the end of this period, there is still no sign that the repairs will be carried out, you may go ahead with them yourself, taking the cost from your rent. Keep detailed records of everything you've done and a copy of every letter you write and receive. If you are in any doubt, at any stage, seek advice.

Dear Landlord
As I told you by (phone/letter) on (date), the water heater at (the address) is broken, and it is your responsibility to put this right under our tenancy agreement. Since this has not been done, I have got (three) estimates for repairs from (names and addresses of firms), which I enclose. Unless I hear from you by (date) that you will do these repairs straightaway, I will have no option but to ask (name your choice) to do the repair. I shall then deduct their bill from future rental payments.
Yours sincerely,

Eviction

Generally speaking, you cannot be made to leave the house or flat that you are renting, unless the landlord has given you notice in the correct way and obtained a possession order from a court. In most cases, it is a criminal offence for anyone to evict you without a court order, or to try to force you out with threats. Court orders are not necessary, however, if you live in lodgings or your landlord lives on the premises. But your landlord still can't use violence to force you to leave. This is an offence under the *Criminal Law Act 1977*.

If you're threatened with eviction, get advice straightaway from a solicitor or your local council housing department or Citizens Advice Bureau. Make sure you keep on paying the rent. Failure to pay will make it easier for the landlord to require you to leave.

Harrassment If your landlord stops short of physical violence, but still behaves in a way designed to make you leave - like changing the locks, shouting abuse or playing loud music - they will be breaking the *Protection from Eviction Act 1977*. Again your local council, housing advice centre or Citizens Advice Bureau can help. If physical violence is used or threatened, call the police.

■ BRIEF CASE: Laurie

brief case

A few weeks after signing a six-month tenancy agreement for a bed-sit, Laurie was told to leave. His landlord had decided to sell the house and knew he would get more money for it with Laurie out of his room. The lock on Laurie's door was taken off, and the landlord threatened to tip his possessions into a black plastic bag. Without a job, Laurie spent more than two months sleeping in his car. With legal advice, and using legal aid, he took his case to court. The judge decided Laurie had been illegally evicted and ordered the landlord to pay him £36,500 in compensation - the extra amount of money the landlord made by selling his house without a tenant.

Insurance If you are living in rented accommodation, insurance for the building is normally arranged by the owner, but it's worth checking exactly what this covers. Building insurance will not cover the cost of replacing your things if they are damaged or stolen. You can arrange to insure your belongings through an insurance company or a broker, see **money**, pages 58-59.

If you have anything valuable, like a camera, stereo or jewellery, you will need to list it separately on the insurance and find out exactly how much it costs to replace. The same applies to something like a bike that may be stolen or lost outside the home.

Some policies will give you the full replacement cost; others take into account wear and tear, and pay you less. If you are under insured it means that your belongings are insured for less than their real value. If the insurance company discovers this when you make a claim, the amount they pay out is likely to be reduced.

Noisy neighbours The best way to tackle a problem of noise, or any other nuisance, is to talk to the person concerned, if possible, before the situation gets out of hand. Sometimes this is easier and more effective if several people complain together. If this doesn't work, write a simple letter (keep a copy), and allow a reasonable time for your neighbour to respond.

If that fails, get in touch with your local environmental health department. They have powers to investigate and deal with the matter, under the *Environmental Protection Act 1990*. See also **leisure**, page 86.

homelessness

Council help

If you are homeless, the council housing department should be able to help. It has a legal duty to give you advice and help towards finding somewhere to live, but this is not the same as offering you somewhere to stay. The council has to house you only if you are 16 or over and

- **homeless; and**
- **in priority need; and**
- **have a connection with the local area; and**
- **have not made yourself intentionally homeless.**

You should qualify as a priority need if

- **you're pregnant; or**
- **you have a child who depends on you; or**
- **you've had to leave your last home because someone was violent towards you; or**
- **you've lost your home through something like a fire or flood; or**
- **your age, health problems or disability makes you vulnerable and unable to cope with being homeless.**

If you are 16 or 17, or under 21 and were in care before you were 18, you will be treated as a priority need. If you have recently left care you are entitled to suitable accommodation until you are 18. Seek advice from Shelter or other housing advice centres.

Sleeping rough

This is dangerous, and places the person at risk of being assaulted. Without an address, it is harder to get a job and even benefit. Under the *Vagrancy Act 1824*, someone found sleeping rough or begging more than once may be fined. Under new law people who sleep rough can be given an anti-social behaviour order, and face prison if they continue to break the law.

SQUATTING

A squatter is someone who enters and occupies land, or any part of a building, without the owner's permission. Squatting is not a crime, but squatters may commit an offence if they cause damage when getting into the property or to the contents, or by using gas or electricity without first making the proper arrangements.

If squatters leave a place empty, the owner can break in and take possession, but commits an offence if force is used while the squatters are still inside. An owner or tenant who intends to move in immediately and use the property as a place of residence, may use reasonable force in getting a squatter to leave, but normally requires a written statement or certificate showing that the property is needed as a home. In this situation a squatter commits an offence in refusing to leave.

Squatters can also be evicted from a property through the issue of a possession order by a court. There are a number of different types of order but, in some circumstances, squatters may have only 24 hours to leave and may not return to the property within the next twelve months.

Advice is available for anyone considering squatting, see **contacts**.

leisure

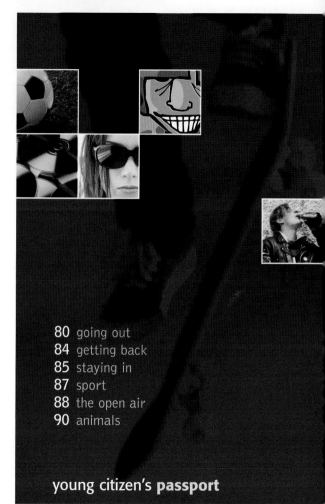

young citizen's **passport**

INDIVIDUALS ENGAGING IN SOCIETY — Citizenship Foundation

going out

It may be for fun, but you don't leave your legal rights at home when you go out for the night. If you spend an evening at a match or concert looking at nothing more than a roof support or girder, then you have a right to complain and ask for a refund. It's no excuse for the management to say that you should have arrived earlier for a better seat. Under the law of contract they should have warned you that the view was restricted before selling you the tickets.

There is no simple law setting out people's rights in the event of a change to the advertised programme or the cancellation of a performance. Your legal position will depend on such things as advance publicity, information given when the ticket was sold and the circumstances that forced a change of plan.

Although disgruntled spectators have been successful in taking promoters to court, legal action is not recommended for disappointment over a cancelled event. Some promoters will try to retain goodwill by offering tickets for another performance, or refunds. If they don't, it's worth explaining why you think their action is unreasonable - a key word in cases of this kind.

Pubs and off-licences

The licensing laws controlling the sale of drinks were introduced in the First World War, and it's only in the last few years that they have begun to change.

Providing they sell soft drinks and food, pubs can now apply for a children's certificate allowing children under 14, accompanied by an adult, into a bar. The children, however, have to leave by 9pm.

Once you're 14, it's legal for you to go into the bar of a pub, but only for soft drinks and at the licensee's discretion. At 16, or over, you can buy beer, cider or perry (made from pear juice), but only to drink with a meal in the dining or restaurant area of a pub.

Only when you're 18 can you buy alcohol or drink alcohol in a bar. Drinks with 0.5% or less of alcohol, such as some canned shandy and low alcohol beers, are treated as non-alcoholic. It is an offence to sell alcohol to anyone under 18 - unless it can be shown that the landlord did their best to check the person was 18 or over. It's also an offence for you to buy, or try to buy, alcohol if you are under 18, or to buy or try to buy it for someone under 18. The maximum fine for this is £1,000, and licensees stand to lose their licence after more than one conviction.

The measures of alcohol that you can be sold are legally controlled. A reasonable head forms part of a pint of beer unless the glass has a line measure. The prices of drinks and food should be displayed by law, and should be clearly visible from where the drinks are served.

REFUSING TO SERVE

Pubs and off-licences can refuse to serve anyone with drink who looks as if they've had enough already, otherwise they can be charged with 'permitting drunkenness' and fined. Licensees have the right to ban or refuse to serve anyone they choose - unless it is because of their sex, religion, ethnic group or disability.

use the law with care **try talking first**

Not in public If a young person under 18 is in a public place (eg the street), or a place they have entered illegally, and have been drinking, or are about to drink, the police or another accredited person can, under the *Confiscation of Alcohol (Young Persons) Act 1997*, require them to stop drinking and can take away the alcohol. Refusal may lead to arrest or a fine of up to £500.

They can also take alcohol from someone over 18 who is in a public place, if they believe it will be passed to under-age drinkers.

The police can ask for the name and address of anyone from whom they have taken alcohol in these circumstances, and it is an offence to refuse to give these details or to give a false name and address.

In some parts of the country, it is against the law for anyone to drink alcohol in public.

Proof of age If you have trouble proving you are over 18, you can apply for a proof of age card, carrying your name, photograph, date of birth and signature. The largest scheme is run by the Portman Group - an organisation sponsored by Britain's major drinks companies - and a card costs £5. Application forms are available online or from pubs, off-licences and supermarkets. See **contacts**.

Eating out

Quality

Whether you're in an expensive restaurant or an ordinary takeaway you have the right to reject any food of a quality below the standard that you are reasonably entitled to expect. What is 'reasonable' depends on such things as the price charged, what the menu says, and basic standards. The laws applying to faulty goods or services also apply. See **money**, page 48-51).

Complaints It's advisable to complain as soon as you know there's a problem and before eating food you believe is unsatisfactory. The more you are paying the higher the standard you're entitled to expect.

If the quality of your meal is poor or the service is bad, you are entitled to make a reasonable deduction from the bill, but don't leave without paying. Explain to the manager why you are not satisfied, and leave your name and address. It is then up to the restaurant to take this up with you later on if they wish.

Price All restaurants, pubs and cafés must, by law, clearly display the price of food and drink where it is served, so you can read it before you order or sit down at a table.

Service charge A service charge may sometimes be added to the bill in a restaurant. It is usually around ten per cent. If it was made clear before you ordered that service will be included, then you have got to pay it. If the service was unsatisfactory, see the manager to ask for a discount. If there is no service charge included, it is up to you whether to leave a tip.

Safety Under the *Food Safety Act 1990*, it is an offence for a restaurant to serve food that is unfit for human consumption. If you are concerned about the hygiene in a place where you have eaten, you can contact your local environmental health office, which has the power to investigate.

Raves

Anyone who organises a rave needs an entertainment licence. To get one the event must meet certain safety standards. Many raves are legal and are arranged in conjunction with the local licensing authorities. Unlicensed raves are illegal.

Under the *Criminal Justice and Public Order Act 1994*, the police have the power to break up an unlicensed open air rave of more than 100 people if the noise and disturbance are likely to cause distress to local people. Under the direction of a senior police officer, the police can order off the land anyone who is preparing, waiting for, or attending the rave. They can also seize and confiscate any sound equipment. Anyone who goes back onto the land within seven days can be fined or imprisoned for up to three months. The police can also stop anyone within five miles of the rave, and order them not to proceed to the gathering. Anyone who refuses to turn back may be fined.

Although the police have the powers to close raves and unlicensed parties that break the law, many forces prefer to get involved only if there is a danger to people's safety or a serious nuisance.

Drugs

Despite the drug culture that surrounds raves the possession of drugs remains illegal and can lead to a criminal record, a fine and imprisonment. In addition taking Ecstasy causes a rise in body temperature. Coupled with the heat inside the building, there is a serious danger of dehydration or heatstroke if body fluid is not replaced. It's advisable to drink about a pint of water every hour and to take regular breaks. Alcohol doesn't help, as it dehydrates the body even further. For more information on drugs and the law, see **life**, page 10.

GAMBLING

Anyone under 18 is forbidden from going into a casino, betting shop, private club, or into an amusement arcade with gaming machines offering all cash prizes of £10 or more.

Lottery tickets or scratch cards should not be sold to anyone under 16 and winnings cannot be collected by someone below this age.

If you're under 18, you are only allowed into a licensed bingo club if you don't take part.

Gambling contracts cannot be enforced in law. If the loser fails to pay, he or she cannot be taken to court. Therefore, if you bet, it's wise to use a reputable bookie.

Nightclubs

Nightclubs must have special licences for entertainment and the sale of alcohol. Like pubs, it's illegal to sell alcohol to someone under 18, and owners are within their rights to choose who they will or will not allow in, as long as they do not break the anti - discrimination laws. Clubs who charge lower entry fees for women than men are breaking the law.

The door

Bouncers have no special legal powers. The same laws apply to them as everyone else, which means that they can only use a reasonable amount of force to throw someone out. In certain circumstances this means no force at all - and a bouncer who uses too much force without good reason commits an offence.

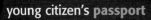

Black cabs, licensed taxis

These are under tight licensing control. The vehicles must be checked regularly, the fares are set by law and the drivers may have had to sit an exam to get their licence. Black cabs can be flagged down, as well as hired, from a taxi rank. From a rank a taxi driver cannot unreasonably refuse to take a fare. It is a criminal offence for a driver of a cab to lengthen the journey in time or distance without cause.

Under the *Disability Discrimination Act 1995*, newly licensed taxis in most areas have to be fully accessible to disabled travellers. Black cab and licensed taxi drivers are also required to help disabled people in and out of taxis and to help with their luggage - although drivers can claim exemption from these regulations if they have a back injury that prevents them from lifting heavy objects.

Minicabs, private hire cars

All minicabs, private hire cars and their drivers must be licensed by the local authority. If you want a private hire car, you should either book it in advance or wait in the cab office. Even if there's a meter, it's a good idea to get an estimate of the fare before you set off. If there's not,

always agree the fare in advance. Minicabs and private hire cars are generally unaffected by the *Disability Discrimination Act*.

Unlicensed taxis

Unlike black cabs or licensed taxis, these vehicles will not have been specially examined and may not even have a current MOT. They will not be insured to carry fare paying passengers. So passengers have little protection if anything goes wrong.

No entry

The driver of a licensed taxi or hire car who without good reason refuses to take a passenger (including a disabled person) may be prosecuted and fined under the *Town Police Clauses Act 1847*. Anyone who feels that they are a victim of this, and wishes to do something about it, should make a note of the plate or registration number of the taxi or hire vehicle and report it to their local licensing authority. (The main local council switchboard can provide the number.) The licensing authority will investigate the case and then prosecute the driver if they feel there is sufficient evidence.

use the law with care try talking first

Parties

Drink and drugs

Although you can't buy alcohol from an off-licence until you're 18, anyone over five can drink alcohol on private premises. It is an offence to give alcohol to a child under five, unless given by a doctor or in an emergency.

An offence is committed, under the *Misuse of Drugs Act 1971*, if you knowingly allow anyone into your flat or house to supply an illegal drug to someone else, or allow the smoking of cannabis. Even if you are not taking the drug yourself, you can still be charged, as it is your place they are using. The penalty for someone allowing their flat or house to be used for drug-taking is up to 14 years in prison for a Class A or B drug, or five years for a Class C drug. For more on the law and drugs, see **life** pages 10-12.

Safety

You invite some friends around for the evening and one of them falls down the stairs. If the cause of the accident was the state of the carpet rather than too much beer, you or your parents could be liable for their injuries. This doesn't mean wrapping every sharp corner in cotton wool, but something like a loose piece of stair carpet definitely should be fixed, since it is reasonable for visitors to expect to walk down the stairs safely. You're not expected to guard against the unforeseeable. If someone slides down the banisters and breaks a leg, then that's their problem.

Insurance

If someone is injured in your home you could be required to pay them compensation - although this can be paid through an insurance policy, if you have one. Most householders' insurance policies cover owners for injuries to other people called "third parties" caused by the state of the buildings or its fittings. If you're in rented accommodation, your landlord could be liable - and again it is his or her insurance company that would pay damages. If you face this problem you can check with a solicitor or Citizens Advice Bureau.

Gatecrashing

Gatecrashing is trespass. The law says that you can use reasonable force to get gatecrashers to leave, but don't start waving a broken bottle around. This is unreasonable and will leave you in more trouble than them.

staying in

Noise If there is a noisy party and the police are called, they can ask people to be quiet, but there's not much else they can do unless they fear there's going to be a breach of the peace - that is some kind of disorder. Then arrests will almost certainly be made.

However, if you are being disturbed by noise from a neighbour between 11pm and 7am, you can ring the local environmental health department, which must investigate your complaint as soon as possible. Under the *Noise Act 1996*, they have the power to send an officer to the house to measure the noise and decide whether it is excessive. If it is, the person believed to be responsible will be given a warning notice, requiring the noise to be switched off or turned down within ten minutes. An offence is committed if the noise continues, the officer can decide to prosecute or issue an on the spot fine of £100. If an on the spot fine is paid within 14 days no further legal action can be taken for the offence; if it is not paid, a court can impose a higher fine.

If the warning notice is ignored, the officer can also obtain a warrant (often very quickly) to go into the building and remove the sound equipment that is being used.

For other problems with noisy neighbours, see **home**, page 77.

TV, video, music and games A licence is required if anyone in a household uses a TV, video recorder and/or any other television apparatus such as a television enabled computer. One licence covers all the equipment in a single home. If rooms are rented separately, a license must be obtained for the TV equipment in each room. A licence will also cover a television powered by batteries used by a full-time student living away from home.

Copyright Copyright laws give writers, artists, publishers etc. the right to take action against anyone who makes a copy of, or broadcasts their work without permission. Breaking copyright is not a criminal offence and the law is only usually enforced against people who are making illegal copies in large numbers or to sell.

Books, plays, films and music written or made since 1 August 1989 are protected by copyright law for 70 years after the author's death (50 years if created before then). Computer generated work and broadcasts are covered for 50 years from the time they were made.

You can make a tape of a TV or radio broadcast for your own use, but only so you can listen to it at a more convenient time. Strictly speaking, it's against the law to record a programme if you intend to keep it as part of a collection or because you find it particularly interesting or enjoyable. Copying a CD, tape or computer game belonging to someone else is also illegal.

BRIEF CASE

The EasyInternetCafé burned CDs of internet downloads(including MP3 music) on behalf of their customers and for profit. Some of the downloads were Sony's copyright and they successfully sued the Café to stop it being done.

Safety

It's an offence to be drunk at a football match or to have alcoholic drinks in the ground, and even on a supporters' coach or train travelling to or from the event. At the moment the law only applies to football.

Risks and the duty of care

Anyone who plays sport must expect to suffer the sorts of injuries normal to the game concerned. But intentional or reckless damage to someone else is another matter, and the player responsible can be sued for damages and prosecuted for a criminal offence. Organisers of sporting events also have a duty to see that visitors, spectators and passers-by are reasonably safe.

BRIEF CASE: Football

A Stockport County player was awarded £250,000 after his career was ended through injuries suffered in a match against Swansea City. The court decided that he was brought down by a tackle aimed at the legs, rather than the ball, which did not reflect the reasonable care that players should show towards one another.

Banned

Under the *Football (Disorder) Act 2000*, a court can ban a person from attending domestic or international football matches. They can be required to report to a police station before a match and to surrender their passport if banned from an international game.

the open air

All land in the United Kingdom is owned by someone - private landowners, a local authority, government body (eg Ministry of Defence), or the Crown, (the Queen). You will not usually end up in court by stepping on to a piece of land marked "trespassers will be prosecuted". Trespass is not a crime (unless you also cause damage) - it's a civil offence. A landowner can require the trespasser to leave, but in doing so may use only a reasonable amount of force. If the trespasser refuses to go, the landowner should call the police.

Footpaths

If a route across a piece of land has been used for 20 years or more without interruption, that route becomes a right of way. A footpath cannot be lost through disuse. Once a right of way has been established it can be used forever unless it is closed by an order made under the *Highways Act 1980* or the *Town and Country Planning Act 1990*.

Strictly speaking, footpaths are for walkers only. It's a criminal offence to drive a motorbike or car on a path. Footpaths are shown on Ordnance Survey maps - but if you need to check on a path, you can ask to look at the maps in the local council planning office.

Under the *Rights of Way Act 1990*, when land is ploughed or any crop (except grass) is planted over a public footpath, the landowner must, within 14 days, make sure that the line of the path is clear to anyone using it. It is also an offence to put up a misleading sign, such as "private" that discourages people from using a public right of way. If you come across a problem of this kind and want something done, contact the local council.

The local council's Rights of Way Officer has a duty to make sure that public rights of way are kept open and free from obstruction. It's the local council's responsibility to maintain footpaths so that people can walk along them, and the job of the landowner to look after stiles and gates along the path,

footpath, or bridleway.

The *Countryside and Rights of Way Act 2000*, provides a "right to roam" on land designated as open country. Landowners can impose restrictions on how the land is accessed or used (eg dogs to be on a lead). You can check with the Countryside Agency to see which land is open, see **contacts**.

BULLS

Checking your legal rights here needs some farming knowledge and the ability to tell one breed of bull from another without getting too close. All dairy bulls (breeds like Friesian, Guernsey and Jersey) are banned from fields crossed by public paths. Other types of bull are allowed only if they are in with cows or

heifers, which apparently makes them much less aggressive.

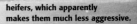
use the law with care try talking first

Rivers, canals and the sea

There is a public right to use a canoe or boat only on the tidal section of a river. Beyond this point you need permission from the owner of the riverbank to use the river.

You also need a licence to use a boat or canoe on a canal - obtainable from British Waterways (the number of your local office will be in the phone book) and the British Canoe Union.

Anyone is free to use a boat or to water-ski or jet-ski on the sea although, in harbours, ferries and other shipping have a right of way.

Fishing

You can fish in the sea and in tidal waters at any time, unless there are local by-laws forbidding it. Fishing off a pier usually needs a licence. Anyone aged twelve or over who fishes for salmon, trout, freshwater fish or eels must have an Environment Agency Rod Fishing Licence, available from post offices or online from the Environment Agency website: see **contacts**. The licence covers England and Wales. Permission is also required from the landowner or the person owning the fishing rights.

Pollution

The Environment Agency asks members of the public to report any environmental incident - on rivers, lakes, canals or the coastline - or the dumping of rubbish, by ringing their local Environment Agency office (in the phone book) or by calling 0845 9 333 111.

Beaches

Land between the low and high tide lines is the property of the Crown - but there is almost never a problem in walking along a beach. However, there is no right to get onto a beach over private land, unless there is a public right of way.

BRIEF CASE: Katrina

Katrina noticed that the water in Ackhurst Brook near Wigan, where she lived, was an unusual colour - particularly around the discharge pipe used by a local factory. She rang the Environment Agency who sent an officer to investigate. The officer reported that the water was discoloured and smelt foul and contained pieces of food that looked like shells from baked beans - which is just what they were. The company admitted polluting the river and was fined £5,000 by local magistrates.

brief case

animals

The *Wildlife and Countryside Act 1981* protects a wide range of wild animals, birds and plants and covers killing, injuring, taking or possessing and disturbing their place of shelter or protection. For an up-to-date list of protected species, see Whitakers Almanack, available in most libraries and the RSPB website. *The Wild Mammals (Protection) Act 1996* makes it an offence to inflict unnecessary suffering on any wild mammal.

Under the *Pet Animals Act 1951* it is an offence to sell a pet animal to anyone below the age of 12. Under the *Protection of Animals Act 1911*, a pet owner has a legal responsibility to care for the animal and make sure it does not suffer unnecessarily. It is an offence to be cruel to the animal or to abandon it if it is likely to cause the animal unnecessary suffering.

Pet owners are also responsible for any damage their animal causes if they knew (or should have known) it was likely to cause such damage, or if their animal is defined as dangerous.

Dangerous animals are known, in law, as those that are not domesticated in this country and might be expected to have dangerous characteristics, such as a monkey or snake. Anyone keeping an animal of this kind must have a licence.

Under the *Control of Dogs Order 1992*, anyone owning a dog must make sure that it wears a collar with the name and address of its owner when it is in a public place. If a dog fouls a footpath, the person in charge of the dog commits an offence if he or she fails to clear up the mess.

It is an offence under the *Dangerous Dogs Act 1991*, to allow a dog to be dangerously out of control in a public place. The owner, or person in charge, of the dog can be fined or imprisoned for up to six months. The court can also order the dog to be destroyed, and can disqualify the owner from keeping a dog in the future. A farmer is allowed to shoot a dog that is not under anyone's control and is worrying livestock on their land.

Under the *Guard Dog Act 1975*, guard dogs should be under the control of a handler or else tied up and prevented from roaming freely. A warning notice should also be displayed. The Act does not apply to dogs guarding private houses or farmland.

▦ BRIEF CASE: Lisa

When Lisa had to go away unexpectedly, she said that she asked a friend to feed and water her pet rat, Ziggy. After Lisa had been gone for six days, one of Lisa's neighbours told the RSPCA that the animal was in need of care. They found the rat with just a scrap of cheese and no water. It was dehydrated, trembling, and close to death. Lisa, who was unemployed, was fined £80 and told to pay £50 towards the cost of the case.

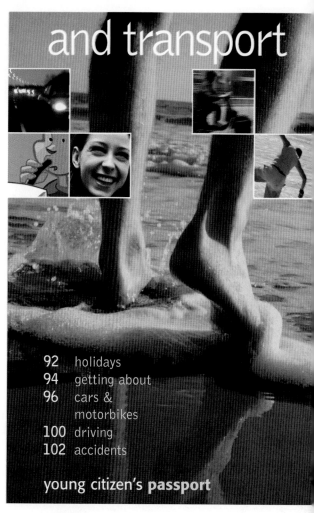

travel
and transport

young citizen's **passport**

INDIVIDUALS ENGAGING IN SOCIETY

Citizenship Foundation

holidays

Package holidays

When you book a holiday, you are making a contract with the tour organiser - that is the company responsible for arranging the package. This is usually the tour operator, but it can also be the travel agent, particularly if you have asked for extra arrangements to be made, not included in the brochure.

Although holiday brochures are designed to show the hotel or resort at its best, the *Package Travel, Package Holidays and Package Tours Regulations 1992* state that they must be accurate and not misleading. If the room or the swimming pool that you were promised is not available, you may be able to claim compensation because of the failure of the company arranging the holiday to keep its side of the contract. It is an offence, under the *Trade Descriptions Act 1968*, for a firm to make a statement that it knows to be false about the goods or services it provides. Prosecutions for this are usually made by local trading standards officers.

It's important to tell the travel agent or tour operator if you have any special needs at the time you make the booking.

Before you sign or hand over any money, read the small print and to check what it says about changes to your schedule. Under certain circumstances, travel organisers can alter flight times or accommodation arrangements provided they make this clear in the brochure or contract. If you pay all or part of the cost of the holiday by credit card, you may be entitled to claim a full or partial refund from the credit card company if the firm organising the holiday fails to keep its side of the contract. For more information on paying by credit card, see **money** page 54.

BEFORE YOU GO

- Check whether you need to have any vaccinations, and think about getting medical insurance, see below.
- If you are travelling in the European Union, get Form E111 at a main post office - allowing you free or reduced medical costs - and take the form with you on holiday.
- Check your passport is up to date and whether you need a visa for the country you are visiting. Passports are not needed for travel

to the Republic of Ireland.
- If you're thinking of hitching, check on advisability before you go. In some countries it is illegal.

If you need to know more about travel requirements or conditions, ring the embassy of the country concerned, or visit the Foreign & Commonwealth Office website at www.fco.gov.uk or telephone their Travel Advice line on 020 7008 0232/0233.

use the law with care try talking first

TRAVEL AND MEDICAL INSURANCE

Travel insurance will protect you from losses while you're away and even illness before you go.
Take the policy with you on holiday, so that if anything goes wrong you can make sure you keep to the terms of the agreement.

If you go abroad, book through a travel company registered with ABTA, IATA or ATOL. If the travel firm belongs to one of these organisations, you'll find their symbol in the brochure. They will cover the cost of getting you home, or compensate you for your losses if the company you've booked with goes bust while you're away, or before you've left.

Passports Everyone who travels abroad, including young children, must have their own passport. However, children already included on someone else's passport before October 1998 can continue to travel abroad with the passport holder until either the child reaches 16, the passport expires or the passport is submitted for amendment.

A passport for someone aged 16 or older costs £42 and is valid for ten years, for travel to any country of the world. A passport for someone under 16 costs £25 and is valid for five years.

If something goes wrong If there is a problem with the holiday that the travel company has provided, tell them or their representative as soon as possible. If you're still not satisfied, make a note of the facts (photographic evidence may be helpful), and then contact the travel firm as soon as you get home.

If you're not satisfied with their reply, write to the managing director of the travel firm. If the company belongs to ABTA, you can have your claim decided by an independent person called an arbitrator. If this is not possible, get advice from the Citizens Advice Bureau and, if necessary, a solicitor. Going to court is a last resort.

If your luggage doesn't arrive, report the loss immediately. Try to obtain a copy of any reports that you complete. Under international law, the airline is responsible for lost or damaged luggage, but compensation is paid by weight rather than value, and the airline will not be responsible for fragile items. It may be better to claim through your holiday insurance.

If you lose all your cash and your cards, you can go to a bank and arrange for money to be transferred from home. There will probably be a charge, but it should arrive within 24 hours.

If you lose anything valuable, tell the police and get a note from them confirming that you have done this. Contact the travel company if you lose your ticket home, and immediately report the loss of traveller's cheques or credit cards to the company offices. They often let you reverse the charges for the call. It is very important to report losses to your insurance company within the time limit stated in the policy.

If your passport is lost or stolen, contact the British Consulate who have an office in most big cities and should be able to provide you with help or advice.

In trouble Travellers overseas are automatically subject to the laws of the country they are visiting.

If you're arrested insist on the British Consulate being informed. The Consulate will explain the local procedures, including access to a lawyer and the availability of legal aid. A European Union (EU) national can go to any EU Consulate. See **europe** page 128.

Taking a car or motorcycle

You'll normally need to get a Green Card from your insurance company, which extends your motor insurance to countries other than Great Britain.

It is also worth checking with a motoring organisation who will advise you whether you need an International Driving Permit (AA, RAC and Green Flag will tell you if need an IDP and can issue one too).

If you're driving to Spain, you should also take out a Bail Bond (fianza). Under Spanish law, the car and driver can be detained after an accident, but can be released on production of a Bail Bond. The Bond will also help cover the cost of any legal action or fine. Contact your motor insurance company for both the Green Card and Bail Bond.

If you have an accident, tell the police and ask for a record or receipt. It will help with your insurance claim when you get home. For the same reason, it's also a good idea to take notes and photographs of the incident, including pictures of the number plates of the vehicles involved.

Don't sign anything in a language that you don't understand. If you're put under pressure, write "I don't understand" immediately above your signature.

Coming home

If you are returning from a country within the EU, you do not have to pay customs charges on any goods you bought in that country, but nor can you obtain any duty-free concessions. However, there is generally no limit on the amount you can bring in – as long as the goods are for a gift or your own use.

Limits are, however, placed on alcohol and tobacco and anyone who exceeds these must convince the customs that the goods are not going to be sold on. No one under 17 is entitled to a tobacco or alcohol allowance.

Customs officials can check your baggage for prohibited goods or to see if you need to pay any tax or duty if you have been to a country outside the EU. Details of the powers and duties of customs officers are given in the Traveller's Charter, available from libraries and the Customs website: www.hmce.gov.uk/public/travel

Buses and trains

Tickets

By the time you're 16, you have to pay full fare on all buses and trains, trams and the Underground. In some areas full fare is charged on buses from the age of 14.

If you travel on a train or the London Underground without a ticket, you may be charged an on the spot penalty, as well as the cost of your fare. Information about this is displayed in stations where this system is in operation.

If you are stranded at a station without any money for a ticket, your ticket can be bought for you by someone else at another station, with the authorisation sent by telephone to where you are waiting. This is known as a silk arrangement.

Some tickets are cheaper when travelling outside the rush hour, and travel cards give you further reductions.

use the law with care try talking first

TRAVEL

- A Young Persons Railcard costs
£18 (2003 prices) and entitles you
to a third off most ticket prices.
Everyone aged 16-25 is eligible to
have one, as are full-time
students aged 26 and over. You
can buy the Railcard at large
stations, some travel agents and
from student services at college
or by phone, see contacts.
- An Inter-Rail Pass gives you at
least 12 days' rail travel in
Continental Europe from £125,
with discounts available on
Eurostar and many cross Channel
ferries. You must be under 26, be
a citizen of or have lived in
Europe for at least six months
and have a passport. Inter-Rail
cards are available from selected
stations and travel agents.
- Student /Young Persons
Discount Coachcards entitle
young people aged 16-25, and
fulltime students students over
25, to a 30% discount on UK
coach journeys. One year cards
cost £10, and £19 buys a card
valid for three years.
- The Under 26 International
Youth Card and the Euro<26 card
provide members with discounted
air fares worldwide, and also
offers reductions on places to
stay and visit. See contacts.

COMPLAINTS

If your train (or bus) is late, there's not
a lot in law that you can do about it.
When you buy a ticket, you have no
legal guarantee that the train will run
on time (or even at all), or that you'll
have a seat when it does come. All
this is explained in the small print,
known as the conditions of carriage,
which can be checked at station ticket
offices.

Under the Passengers' Charter you
may be offered 20% of the ticket price
in compensation if you're stuck on a
train that has been seriously delayed,
for one hour or more, or if you have a
season ticket for a train service that
has been below the standard set for
punctuality or reliability.

If you have a complaint about a train
service, you can ask for a complaints
form at a station or write to the
customer relations manager for the
route you have travelled on.

■ BRIEF CASE: Emma

Emma bought a ticket for a day trip to
London, saying that she wanted to
travel on the next train, leaving in 15
minutes. When the inspector checked her
ticket on the train, she asked Emma to pay
a further £6, as she had been undercharged
by the booking clerk. Although Emma
claimed that it was the train operating
company's mistake in selling her the wrong
ticket, by law she had to pay the difference.
When a contract is made, one side cannot
gain by the other side's genuine mistake.

young citizen's **passport**   95

Getting started

It is an offence to drive or ride a motor vehicle without the correct licence. You get a full driving licence when you have passed your test, and the licence will be valid until you are 70. Licences for drivers over 70 are issued for three years at a time.

New licences are now the size of a credit card and contain the holder's photograph. Old paper licences will be changed to the new format when they are renewed or if the details need to be changed. You must tell DVLA (see **contacts**) of any change of address immediately - or risk a fine.

If you want to learn to drive, you need a provisional driving licence. Application forms are available from post offices. When you get your licence, sign it immediately - don't drive until you have done so. Car drivers can hold the same provisional licence until they are 70. A motorcyclist's provisional licence is only valid for two years.

Learning to drive a car

When you are driving on a provisional licence you must display 'L' plates ('D' plates in Wales), which should be removed or covered up when the vehicle is not being driven by a learner. You must not drive on a motorway, and you must have someone with you in the front passenger seat of the car who is over 21 and has held a full EU driving licence for three years. This person must be fit to drive and must not have had more than the legal amount of alcohol.

The driving test is in two parts, a written theory exam and a practical test. The theory paper, which must be passed before taking the practical test, lasts 40 minutes and is made up of 35 multiple-choice questions. Driving test theory papers are now conducted by computer, with results given in half an hour.

Learning to ride a motorcycle, moped or scooter

Motorcyclists also have to take a theory paper and a practical test to gain a licence, unless they already have a full car licence, when only the practical test is required. Before you can ride a motorcycle on the road, you must successfully complete a Compulsory Basic Training course, unless you had a full car licence on 1st February 2001 and only want to ride a moped (with an engine of up to 50cc and a maximum speed of no more than 30mph).

Motorcyclists must learn on a machine no larger than 125cc. After passing the practical test, they are restricted for two years to bikes with a power output of up to 25 kw or 33 bhp, after which they may ride any size of bike. Riders over the age of 21 who don't want to wait this long to ride a larger bike can choose to take further tests, known as direct and accelerated access. See **contacts**.

Learner motorcyclists may not ride on a motorway, nor carry a pillion passenger, unless the passenger is also licensed to ride that type of machine. Mopeds, scooters, and motorised skateboards cannot be used on the public roads without a licence, road tax and insurance.

use the law with care try talking first

MOT

Most vehicles that are three or more years old must pass an MOT test if they are to be used or left on the road.

Road tax

A car or motorbike must display a current tax disc, whether it is being used or just standing on the road. The fine for breaking this regulation is normally about twice the cost of the disc. The Driving and Vehicle Licensing Agency (usually known as the DVLA), now have powers to wheel clamp and remove vehicles not showing a current disc, and to charge a fee for their release. It is a crime to use a tax disc belonging to another vehicle.

If you have a vehicle that you take off the road (eg for repairs) and decide not to tax, you must inform the DVLA on the reminder form sent to you when the vehicle licence is due for renewal. The penalty for not doing this is a fine of up to £1,000.

Insurance

It is an offence to drive, ride or even place a motor vehicle on the road without insurance. The penalties for this are very heavy, and it makes no difference for someone to say it was a genuine mistake and that they thought they were insured. Failure to have insurance means a fine and penalty points on a licence, and possible disqualification.

It is also an offence for someone to allow their car or motorcycle to be used by a person who is not insured to drive it.

There are three different kinds of motor insurance, offering different levels of cover:

- **third party insurance only pays for damage caused to other people or their property (and not to your own vehicle). This is the minimum level of insurance cover required by law;**
- **third party fire and theft gives you further protection by covering your vehicle against theft or fire damage;**
- **fully comprehensive insurance is usually the most expensive, but covers the cost of accident repair damage to your vehicle as well as compensating you and others for injuries or damage in the accident.**

When you apply for any insurance, make sure the information you give is accurate and complete. If it's not, your insurance will be invalid. It's an offence knowingly to make a false statement to obtain insurance. For more information, see **money**, page 58.

■ BRIEF CASE: Sarah

Sarah bought a Morgan sports car, and insured it for her and her fiancé to drive. The car, worth £26,000, was stolen. When she claimed on her insurance, it came to light that her fiancé had received a serious motoring conviction several years ago, which Sarah had failed to mention on the application form. The insurance policy was therefore not valid, and Sarah received no compensation for the loss of her car.

cars and motorbikes

AT WHAT AGE?

At 14 you can ride an electrically powered pedal cycle.

At 16 you can ride a moped up to 50cc, a small tractor, mowing machine or invalid car. If you receive a disability living allowance, at the higher rate, you can also drive a car.

At 17 you can drive a car with up to 8 passenger seats, a motor tricycle, a motorbike up to 125cc, a large tractor and a van or lorry up to 3.5 tons.

At 18 you can drive a van or lorry up to 7.5 tons.

At 21 you can drive all other vehicles. For hiring a car, most car hire companies have a minimum age of 21 or 23.

Traffic offences

Every vehicle on the road must meet a whole set of regulations covering brakes, tyres, lights, mirrors, steering and even windscreen washer bottles (which must, by law, never be empty). A police officer may stop a vehicle at any time to check that it is in roadworthy condition, and it is no excuse for the driver to claim that they didn't realise a light wasn't working. These are absolute offences and apply even if the driver was completely unaware of the problem.

If the police believe a vehicle is not roadworthy, they can instruct the driver to get it checked and repaired by a garage (usually within 14 days), give the driver a fixed penalty or call up a specially trained vehicle examiner to inspect the car or bike there and then. A police officer who feels a vehicle is so dangerous that someone will probably be injured if it is used any further, can immediately ban it from being driven.

Cycling

Cyclists are expected to follow the same basic laws as other road users. They have a duty of care to pedestrians, other riders and road users. It is an offence, under the *Highways Act 1835*, to ride a bicycle (or tricycle) on the pavement - a law that applies to riders of all ages. Police officers now have the power to impose a £20 fixed penalty fine on cyclists who ride on the pavement. It is also against the law to wheel a bike past a red traffic light or to ride it across a zebra crossing.

It is an offence to ride under the influence of alcohol or drugs. There is no breath test for cyclists; a court would instead be guided by evidence from the officer who made the arrest.

BUYING A CAR

- A small popular car is usually less of a risk. Spare parts are cheaper and easier to obtain, insurance costs lower and it will probably be easier to sell when you want to change it.
- A car bought privately is usually cheaper than one bought from a dealer, but you have fewer rights if things go wrong. The *Sale of Goods Act 1979* (see money, page 48), gives greater protection if you buy from a dealer. A car bought privately need only be "as described". The legal expression "caveat emptor" (meaning "buyer beware"), particularly applies when buying a second-hand car. It is notoriously difficult to get problems sorted out once you have paid for the car.
- Look at the car in daylight. Take someone along with you who knows about cars. Check the owner's purchase documents to see if any hire-purchase payments are still due. For between £100-£300 the RAC, AA or Green Flag will inspect and report on the mechanical state of the car, check on the HP payments and tell you whether the car has been stolen or is an insurance write-off. HPI Autodata or AA Car Data provide a similar service at a slightly lower cost, without the mechanical inspection.
- Look to see if the car's mileage tallies with the MOT certificate and the service history. You can also check with previous owners. Ask the dealer if they have tried to verify the mileage - they have to do this by law. Be wary if there is a sticker on the speedometer indicating that there is no guarantee that the mileage is accurate.
- Ask to see the Vehicle Registration Document (V5). If it's a private sale, it should contain the seller's name and address. It also gives the Vehicle Identification Number (VIN), which should correspond with the number stamped on identification plates under the bonnet and on the floor. If you have any doubts, leave the car alone.
- If you buy a car that turns out to be stolen, it remains the property of the true owner - meaning that you will almost certainly lose your money, unless you can get it back from the person from whom you bought the car.

■ BRIEF CASE: Anna

Anna went to look at a Ford Escort, advertised privately in her local paper. She asked the seller if the car had been in an accident. He said no, but having bought the car, Anna later found evidence of major crash repairs. She went back to the seller, pointed out the car was not as described and eventually got her money back. However, if the car had just been unreliable (even breaking down on her first drive), there is probably little she could have done, as there is nothing in law that states that a car bought privately must be of satisfactory or reasonable quality.

Safety

Seat belts and crash helmets

Seat belts (front and rear), where fitted, must be worn by drivers and passengers. If a passenger in your car does not wear a belt, it is he or she who will be prosecuted, not you - unless the passenger is under 14, when it is your responsibility.

Motorcyclist and pillion passengers must both wear an approved safety helmet on all journeys. This regulation does not apply to a follower of the Sikh religion while he is wearing a turban. Dark visors may not be worn at night or when visibility is poor.

SPEED LIMITS

Cars and motorcycles are limited to
- **30 mph in built-up areas, unless marked otherwise,**
- **60 mph on single carriageways,**
- **70 mph on dual carriageways and motorways.**

Speed limits are lower for buses, lorries, and cars towing caravans.

Speeding

Speeding is an absolute offence, which means that it is no defence to say that it wasn't dangerous or that you didn't realise that you were breaking the speed limit. Nor is there much point in denying that you were travelling at the speed the police say you were, unless you can prove it. You will usually be fined and given penalty points.

If you break the speed limit, or are seen by the police to be driving carelessly or dangerously, you must be warned of the possibility of prosecution at the time of the offence or served with a summons within 14 days of the offence. Otherwise you cannot be convicted, unless an accident occurred at the time or immediately after.

Driving badly

Careless driving is to drive in a way that is not how a careful and reasonable driver would behave. Pulling out from a side road without looking is an example of this.

Dangerous driving is to drive in a way that is dangerous to people or property, such as driving very fast through a built-up area or overtaking on a sharp bend. Dangerous driving and causing death by dangerous driving are very serious offences, which courts will punish with fines, disqualification, and imprisonment. If you face such a charge, get in touch with a solicitor straightaway.

Stolen vehicles

Stealing a vehicle to sell on to someone else is theft. Joy-riding, or taking a car to ride around in and then dumping it, is a different offence known as "taking a vehicle without the owner's consent" or TWOC. Both are punishable by a fine or imprisonment.

Joyriding

The *Aggravated Vehicle-Taking Act 1992* gives courts powers to deal with joyriders who drive dangerously and are involved in an accident causing injury and damage. A sentence of up to five years' imprisonment may be imposed, with a year's automatic disqualification from driving.

Mobile phones

Since December 2003 it has been an offence to use a hand held mobile phone when driving whether or not they are driving badly. Motorists can be fined from £30 to £1,000 and collect three penalty points.

use the law with care try talking first

■ BRIEF CASE: Peter

Peter was involved in a crash with a motorcycle. He feared that it was his fault and that he would lose his licence, as he already had a number of penalty points. He persuaded his wife Sophie, who was not in the car at the time, to tell the police that it was she who was driving. A week later they both admitted the deception, but were charged with perverting the course of justice. Peter and Sophie were sentenced to four and two months in prison.

Drinking and driving

Alcohol seriously affects a driver's judgement and reactions. There is no law that limits a driver to a certain number of drinks, such as two pints of beer or one glass of wine, but there is a maximum amount of alcohol that you may have in your body while driving or being in charge of a car. In law, being in charge of a car includes simply sitting in the driving seat of parked car.

The limits The amount of alcohol in a person's body can be measured in their breath, blood, or urine. A driver will be found guilty of drink-driving if they have more than 35 micrograms of alcohol in 100 ml of breath, 80 mg of alcohol in 100 ml of blood, or more than 107 mg of alcohol in 100 ml of urine.

Breath tests The police will carry out a road side breath test to check whether a driver has more than the permitted amount of alcohol in their body. Uniformed police can breathalyse anyone whom they reasonably suspect of driving with excess alcohol, who is involved in a traffic offence or road accident, however minor, even if there is no suspicion of alcohol. A uniformed police officer is also quite entitled to stop motorists at random in order to see whether there is a reasonable suspicion that they have consumed any alcohol. If there is, the officer can go on to ask the motorist to take a breath test.

If the test is positive or the driver refuses a breath test, the driver will be arrested and taken to a police station for further tests.

No escape A driver who fails to blow into the device properly, or refuses to take a test, will still end up with a heavy fine and have his or her licence endorsed with three to eleven penalty points. Courts rarely accept that there are special reasons for drivers being over the limit. Disqualification from driving is almost automatic. A drunken driver who causes someone's death may be sent to prison for up to ten years, and will be disqualified from driving for at least two years.

■ BRIEF CASE: Paul

Paul had had a few drinks when he was phoned by a friend who had run out of petrol, miles from anywhere, with his old and sick mother. Paul got into his car to go and fetch them, but was stopped by the police and breathalysed positive. Although he told the court that it was an emergency, the magistrates still found Paul guilty of drinking and driving, saying that the police, RAC or AA could instead have been called to help.

99% PROOF

driving

Penalty points Courts deal with most motoring offences through a system of penalty points that are entered on a driver's licence. Anyone receiving twelve or more points within a period of three years will almost always be disqualified from driving for at least six months. Details of the points carried for each offence are given in the Highway Code. Drivers who have six or more penalty points on their licence within two years of their test, go back to being a learner until they pass a further test.

accidents

What to do Accidents happen to the most careful of drivers, often through no fault of their own. If you are involved in an accident, there are certain things that you should and should not do.....

- Stop immediately. Try to stay calm, even if people are yelling and screaming at you.
- Check that everyone involved in the accident is OK. If anyone is injured, call an ambulance before you do anything else.
- You must give your name and address and details of your vehicle to anyone who has reasonable need to know them. This includes a police officer at the scene of the accident, anyone who is injured, anyone whose property is damaged and the owner of any animal injured or killed. (This applies to horses, cows, sheep, goats and dogs - but not cats.) If someone is injured, you must also produce your insurance certificate to show that you are properly insured. If you can't do this at the time of the accident, then you must give this information to the police as soon as possible, and certainly within 24 hours. If you don't, you will be committing an offence.
- Make sure you get the name, address, vehicle registration number and insurance details of the other drivers involved.

- Contact your insurance company as soon as possible, and also make a detailed note of everything that happened. This should cover the time of day, weather, light, estimated speeds, position of vehicles before and after the accident, what people said and anything else that you think might be relevant. If you can, take photos before anything is moved, or draw a sketch plan as soon as you feel able to do so.
- Don't drive away without stopping. It is a criminal offence.
- Be cautious if the other driver suggests not calling the police and offers you cash to cover the damage. It might be an offence not to report the accident, and you may find that the damage to your vehicle costs a lot more than you are being offered. If someone is injured in the accident it is an offence not to report it to the police.
- Don't admit it was your fault. You may find later that the other driver was drunk, driving too fast, or without lights - in which case you might not be to blame at all. If you do admit responsibility, your words may end up by being used against you in court and may affect your insurance claim.

police
and courts

young citizen's **passport**

INDIVIDUALS
ENGAGING IN
SOCIETY

Citizenship Foundation

powers and duties

Powers and duties

Most of the information that the police receive comes from the general public. Without this help they could do very little.

Much of the law setting out police powers and duties when investigating crime is contained in the *Police and Criminal Evidence Act 1984*. As part of this, the government publishes guidelines that the police must follow when searching for and collecting evidence. These are known as the Codes of Practice. If they are broken when the police are, say, questioning a suspect, a judge or magistrate may decide that the evidence obtained cannot be used in court, and the police officers concerned may be disciplined.

Copies of the Codes of Practice are available from libraries and at every police station. Anyone questioned by the police has a right to read them.

POLICE DISCIPLINE

Police officers must obey both the law of the land, and their own code of discipline. This discipline code is broken if an officer...
- unreasonably neglects their duty;
- makes a false written or spoken statement;
- misuses their authority, eg through unnecessary violence;
- is rude or abusive;
- is racially discriminatory.

The Police have a legal duty to promote racial equality under the *Race Relations (Amendment) Act 2000*.

stop and search

Stop!

If a police officer stops you in the street, you are entitled to know the officer's name and the police station where they work. You are also entitled to know why the officer has stopped you. It is not acceptable for this to be simply because of your colour, dress, hairstyle or the fact that you might have been in trouble before.

Strictly speaking, you don't have to answer a police officer's questions, but someone who refuses to give their name and address may well find themselves arrested if the officer believes that they have something to hide.

However, if the police suspect that you have committed (or are about to commit) an arrestable offence - such as theft, assault or carrying an offensive weapon - then you must give your name and address, but need not say any more. You have the right not to answer any more questions until you have received legal advice, see page 107.

Stay calm 1 If you're stopped by the police, keep calm and don't overreact. If you're obstructive and rude, you're more likely to be arrested. Staying calm will also help you remember what happened and what was said. If you deliberately mislead the police by giving false information or wasting their time, you risk a fine or even imprisonment.

use the law with care **try talking first**

Search!

People

The police do not have the power to search anyone they choose, but they can search someone (and the vehicle in which they are travelling), who has been arrested or is suspected of carrying...

- **illegal drugs;**
- **stolen goods or goods on which duty has not been paid;**
- **weapons, or anything that might be used as a weapon; or**
- **anything that might be used for theft, burglary, deception, joyriding or the hunting or poaching of animals.**

Any search involving more than a check of your outer clothing should be done out of public view or in a police station or van. If the search requires more than the removal of outer clothing, it should be done by someone of the same sex. The way the search is carried out can depend on what the police are looking for. For example, the police may decide to make an intimate search of someone suspected of carrying drugs - given the possibility that the drugs are being hidden inside the person's body.

Stay calm 2

If you, or the vehicle in which you are travelling, are searched by the police, the officer should state beforehand why the search is taking place and what they expect to find. You have every right to ask for an explanation if this has not been made clear.

If the police search you illegally, they are committing an assault. But if they have good reason, and you refuse, you may be charged with obstruction.

The police should normally make a written record of the search and tell you. You can ask for a copy at any time within the next year.

Special powers

Police powers of search in certain circumstances were extended by the *Criminal Justice and Public Order Act 1994*. If a senior police officer believes that a serious violent incident might take place in the area or that dangerous weapons are being carried, they can give officers the authority to stop any person or vehicle to search for the weapons. This applies even when the constable has no grounds for suspecting that the person stopped might have broken the law. With the authority of an officer of the rank of inspector or above, officers may remove and seize anything covering a person's face if they believe it is being used to hide the person's identity.

If you are stopped in this way, you are entitled to request a written record of the search within a year. Failing to stop when asked by a police officer can result in a fine or even imprisonment.

Property The police do not have the power to enter and search any house or building that they choose. But they are allowed to carry out a search if....

- **they have the agreement of the occupier of the building; or**
- **they have reason to believe they might find someone who has committed an arrestable offence, or to look for relevant evidence in a property that was controlled by someone before they were arrested; or**
- **they have a warrant (or permission) from a court; or**
- **in order to catch an escaped prisoner, save life, prevent serious property damage or to prevent certain kinds of disturbance.**

If possible, the police should explain why they are making the search and should keep a record of whether they needed to use force to get in, any damage caused, and anything they took away. If the search is unlawful, it may be possible to get compensation, but this is not easy.

arrest

When the police make an arrest, they are taking the person under the care and control of the law. This means that for the time being, the suspect loses certain freedoms - such as to go and do as they please - but, in return, has certain rights designed to protect them from unreasonable treatment.

If you are arrested and taken to a police station, you are entitled to…

- **know the reason for your arrest;**
- **see a solicitor;**
- **have someone told where you are;**
- **read a copy of the Codes of Practice, which explain the procedures the police should follow when questioning you.**

You should be given a written note of these rights and cautioned - see page 107.

You can be held by the police if they do not have enough evidence to charge you and they reasonably believe that they can preserve or obtain further evidence by continuing to question you.

You cannot normally be held for more than 24 hours without being charged or released. If a serious offence is being investigated, a senior police officer can authorise your detention for a further twelve hours, which can be extended up to a total of 96 hours with the approval of a magistrates' court.

HELPING THE POLICE WITH THEIR ENQUIRIES

If you are asked to go to a police station to help with enquiries, it's important to know if you are being arrested, or whether the decision to attend is up to you. If you are being asked to go voluntarily, you may refuse - although the police may then decide to arrest you - and then you have to go.

You are entitled to send a message to your family or a friend telling them where you are, and to receive free legal advice from a solicitor, even though you are attending the police station voluntarily.

If you have not been arrested and go to the police station voluntarily, you may leave at any time you wish.

use the law with care try talking first

Legal advice

In almost all circumstances, anyone who has been arrested, or who goes to a police station voluntarily, is entitled to legal advice from the solicitor on duty or one of their own choice. The consultation with the duty solicitor is free and in private.

If you have been arrested or are being questioned about a serious arrestable offence, or if you feel at all unsure about your legal position, it is better not to answer questions (except your name and address) until you have had a chance to speak to a solicitor.

With the approval of a senior officer, the police can delay access to a solicitor chosen by the detained person (but not to the duty solicitor) for up to 36 hours if this might interfere with the evidence, endanger or alert others or hinder the recovery of property obtained as a result of the offence.

Questioning

If you are under 17, the police should not normally interview you without your parent or an "appropriate adult" present. An appropriate adult is someone who knows you such as an adult friend or teacher.

If you have been arrested, you must give the police your name and address, but you have the right after that to stay silent and not answer any further questions. However, the court will be told of this if the case goes to trial, and it may strengthen the case against you. If you refuse to answer questions in court, the magistrates or jury are allowed to take this into account in deciding whether you are guilty.

Under the *Police Reform Act 2000* you are required to give your name and address if you are suspected of anti-social behaviour even if you have not been arrested. There are clear rules governing the way police officers can question a person, which are designed to stop unfair pressure being placed on a suspect.

There should be regular breaks for food and the cell and interview room should be clean, properly heated, ventilated, and lit. Someone who is deaf or has difficulty in understanding English should be given a signer or an interpreter.

If, after questioning, the police decide to arrest you, they should give you written information about your legal rights.

The caution

Once a police officer has reason to believe that you have committed an offence, they must caution you by saying: "You do not have to say anything. But it may harm your defence if you do not mention when questioned something that you later rely on in court. Anything you do say may be given in evidence."

Tape recording Your interview at the police station will probably be recorded on tape. The officer will begin with questions about your name and address.

If the interview is not recorded, notes should be made by the officer concerned. You should normally have the opportunity to see these notes and to sign them if you agree that they are a fair record of what was said.

Fingerprints and photographs The police can take fingerprints of anyone who gives their consent or in certain circumstances without their consent. If the person doesn't co-operate, reasonable force can be used. The police are generally allowed to photograph people charged with a recordable offence but must not use force. Fingerprints and photographs must be destroyed if the person is charged and found not guilty, or not charged at all (unless they admit the offence and are formally cautioned for it, or in the case of photographs, if the person has a previous conviction for a recordable offence).

charge, caution, release

After questioning you, the police must decide what to do next. If there appears to be enough evidence, they can…

- **charge you with the offence; or**
- **send the papers to the Crown Prosecution Service, for them to decide whether to charge you; or**
- **arrange to issue you with a formal caution (if you are 18 or over) or a reprimand or warning (if you are under 18).**

Charged If you are to be charged, you will be given a charge sheet indicating the nature of the offence, when and where you are due to appear in court and the conditions of your bail.

Once you are charged you should not be asked any further questions except in certain specified situations, for example, when new information has come to light.

Bail If you are charged with an offence,

the law states that you should normally be released on bail - unless the police believe you should be held:

- **because they doubt the truth of the name and address that you have given;**
- **for the protection of others, to stop you committing another offence or to stop you interfering in their investigations;**
- **for your own protection (or, if you are under 18, because it is in your own interests); or**
- **to make sure you turn up in court.**

If the police do not release you, you must be brought before a magistrate at the earliest opportunity, who will decide whether you can be released on bail and, if so, what conditions should apply. For example,

you may be required to report to the police station once a week, or to have someone provide a financial guarantee that you will be present in court when required. If the court refuses or applies conditions to bail it must give the reasons for this decision.

A person who is charged with, or already convicted of, murder, attempted murder, manslaughter, rape or attempted rape, will only be given bail if the court deciding the matter considers that there are exceptional circumstances which justify doing so. Courts also need not grant bail if it appears that the defendant was already on bail when the offence was committed.

A formal caution

This is a strong warning from a senior police officer reminding you that you could have been sent to court, and that if you commit further offences, that is almost certainly what will happen. Cautions are not for serious offences and can be given only if the accused admits guilt.

For young offenders (under 18) a first offence will result in a young person being given a reprimand or a warning, or facing criminal charges, depending on the seriousness of the case. After a reprimand, a further offence will lead to a warning or charge. Someone who has received a warning and who offends again will normally be charged.

If the police feel there is not enough evidence to make a charge, they will either decide to take no further action (and the case against you will be dropped) or will delay any decision while further enquiries are made.

COMPLAINTS AGAINST THE POLICE

If you feel that you have suffered, or witnessed police misconduct, you may decide that you want to make an official complaint. This should be done within one year of the incident.

Think about what happened; make sure you are clear what was wrong. If it is a serious matter, it's a good idea to speak to a solicitor or contact your local Citizens Advice Bureau beforehand. The Police Complaints Authority (the PCA - an independent organisation that oversees public complaints against police officers) can give advice on the type of things that you should put into a complaint, and information on how the complaint will be investigated. See Contacts.

You can make your complaint in person, at any police station, or by writing to the Chief Constable of the police force concerned or to the PCA.

In reply, you may get an apology, or an explanation of the officer's conduct. If you are not satisfied with this, or your complaint is of a serious nature, there may be a full investigation supervised by the PCA.

courts

Crown Prosecution Service

The job of investigating a crime and charging a suspect is done by the police, but the decision as to whether to continue with the case and bring it to court is made by the Crown Prosecution Service (CPS). This is an independent prosecuting service, made up of trained lawyers, who decide whether there is a realistic chance of conviction and whether the seriousness of the crime merits a trial. If the answer to either of these questions is "no", the case will be dropped.

It is difficult to predict the amount of time it will take to investigate and bring a case to court. If you are charged with an offence normally heard in a magistrates' court, you should know within six months whether you are to be prosecuted.

In certain areas of the country, experimental limits have been set on the amount of time someone under 18 has to wait between their arrest and first appearance in court (36 days), and between their conviction and sentence (29 days). These limits have not yet been introduced nationally.

Charge or Summons

You will be told of the date and time of your first appearance in court on the police charge sheet or by summons through the post.

If you are 17 or under, your case will normally be heard in a youth court. If you are 18 or over, your first appearance will be in the local adult magistrates' court.

Youth Court

If the accused is under 18, the case must normally be heard in a youth court.

If a young person is charged jointly with an adult the trial may be held in a magistrates' court or, in serious cases such as murder, in the Crown Court.

A youth court is made up of either a District Judge sitting alone, or three magistrates (which must include one man and one woman), trained to deal with cases involving young people.

If the accused is under 16, their parents must attend the court. Parents of 16 or 17 year olds may also be ordered to attend.

Members of the public are not allowed in a youth court to listen to the case, nor can the identity or pictures of any young person concerned in the trial be published in the press.

Magistrates' court

All criminal cases pass through magistrates' courts, in some way or another. Normally three magistrates sit in court. Also known as justices of the peace, they are usually not lawyers, but members of the local community. Magistrates will reach a verdict and pass sentence themselves on all cases involving less serious offences (known as summary offences). More serious cases are dealt with by the Crown Court (with a jury), but before they reach this stage, it is the magistrates' job to decide whether there is enough evidence for the accused to stand trial. There are some offences that can be heard by either a magistrates' or Crown Court, and the accused can decide which to choose.

Crown court

This is the court where more serious offences are heard. A judge takes charge of the hearing to make sure that the evidence is properly presented, but the verdict is reached by the jury. The judge will pass sentence if the defendant is found guilty and is generally able to impose higher sentences than a magistrates' court. The sentence is decided by taking into account any maximum set by law, the circumstances surrounding the case, previous convictions, and possibly the background of the defendant if it is thought to have any bearing on the case.

There are procedures set out to ensure that a young person accused of a crime is not made to feel intimidated by the experience and receives a fair trial.

Age of criminal responsibility

A child under the age of ten who breaks the law cannot be charged with the crime. However, children under ten who are out of control can be made subject to a child safety order (placing them under the supervision of a social worker or a member of a youth offending team) or a care order (taking them into care).

courts

Criminal Defence Service

Help with the cost of legal advice and the presentation of your case in court is provided by the Criminal Defence Service.

If you are charged with an offence, it is important to get legal advice as soon as possible. You may wish to use the solicitor that you saw at the police station, or you can consult another one. Solicitors must hold a contract from the Legal Services Commission (LSC) in order to carry out this work. You can find a contracted firm by phoning the LSC or searching the Community Legal Service website, see **contacts**.

There are different types of help available which your solicitor will be able to explain. If you are to be tried in a magistrates' or the Crown Court you may be able to get help with the cost of a solicitor, and possibly a barrister, preparing and presenting your case. Depending on your income and savings, you may be required to make a contribution towards the cost.

If you find yourself in court without anyone to give you advice, you can ask to see the duty solicitor who can give you free advice and representation on your first appearance. You could also ask the magistrates to delay your case until you've had time to talk to someone, though they will probably want to know why you did not sort it out earlier. It is always best if possible to get advice before you go to court.

The Court Service

If you need to go to court, for example as a witness or juror, and need information on what you can expect or what you might have to do, your local court should be able to help (See Courts in the phone book). Further details are given in the Courts' Charter, see **contacts**.

Juries

The job of a jury, which sits in a Crown Court, is to decide on the facts of a criminal case and on the guilt or innocence of the accused. It is made up of twelve adults, aged between 18-70, who have lived in Britain for a continuous period of five years from the age of 13. They are chosen at random from the local Electoral Register (see page 120), but there are certain categories of people who cannot be selected. These include judges, magistrates, ministers of religion, prison, police and probation officers, anyone on bail or who has been on probation within the last five years, anyone sentenced to prison, detention centre, youth custody or community service within the last ten years.

If you are called as a member of a jury, you will usually be given about six weeks' notice. Although some people, such as MPs, members of the armed forces and the medical profession have the right to be excused, normally it is compulsory. But if there is a strong reason why you are unable to serve - such as exams, a holiday which has been already booked, the care of a relative or major problems at work - then you may be excused or allowed to defer your service until later in the year, although it is important to make this clear as soon as possible.

Jurors are able to claim the cost of travel to Court and a small financial allowance. There is information for jurors on the Court Service websites, see **contacts**.

CONTACTS see pages 134-143 for organisations able to give help & advice

law, government
& human rights

young citizen's **passport**

INDIVIDUALS ENGAGING IN SOCIETY

Citizenship Foundation

making the law

Parliament

Between 50-60 major new laws are passed by Parliament each year. Starting as a Bill, each one must be debated and voted on by the House of Commons and the House of Lords before becoming law. The House of Lords can recommend changes and delay the progress of a Bill, but it can't actually stop it from being passed. The only Bill that the House of Lords can reject is one that tries to extend a Parliament's life beyond five years (the maximum time between general elections) - a protection against power being seized by a dictator. The Government has begun the process of reforming the House of Lords by removing the automatic right of many (but not all) hereditary peers to sit and vote.

After going through both Houses of Parliament, a Bill becomes an Act (or statute) by being given the royal assent by the Queen. Today this is a formality. The last monarch to refuse to approve an Act was Queen Anne in 1707.

Most Bills are put to Parliament by the Government as part of its overall policy. A small number are presented by individual MPs and peers, known as private members' Bills. Few of these become law, as there is only a limited amount of time to debate and vote on them. Most of Parliament's time is spent on Government business. Committees of MPs, known as Select Committees, monitor and question what Ministers and their departments do.

European law

The UK is part of the European Union and has agreed to apply new laws agreed by the member states of the EU. This is explained on pages 132-133.

Courts

When a case comes to court, the magistrates or judge normally apply the law in the same way as courts have done in the past. This is called a system of precedent and ensures that similar cases are dealt with in a consistent way. However, there are times when the circumstances of a case have not arisen before, or when the senior judges decide that existing judgments do not reflect modern society. In these situations, by their decision, judges can create or change the law.

The National Assembly for Wales

Elections for the 60 members who make up the Welsh Assembly take place every four years. All laws for Wales are still passed by Parliament in London, although the Assembly can debate and give its views on issues directly affecting Wales. It also has responsibility for deciding how laws affecting, for example, education, health, industry, agriculture, transport, training, and environment, are put into practice in Wales. Questions of foreign affairs, defence, taxation, social security and broadcasting are decided for the whole of the United Kingdom by the Government in London.

■ BRIEF CASE

A month after separating from his wife, a man broke into her parents house where she was staying and tried to have sex with her against her will. The husband was found guilty of attempted rape and sentenced to five years in prison. He appealed on the grounds that a husband could not be found guilty of raping his wife. The case went up to the House of Lords where it was heard by five senior judges. They decided that the rule that a husband could not rape his wife (which went back to before 1736) should no longer be part of the law, since a husband and wife were now seen as equal partners in marriage. As a result the law was changed and a man who forces his wife to have sexual intercourse against her will may now be guilty of rape.

European Convention on Human Rights

This is an international agreement drawn up by the Council of Europe to protect people's human rights after the horrors of the Second World War. It took effect in 1953 and sets out fundamental rights and freedoms that everybody should have and the limited circumstances when the State may interfere with those freedoms. These include a right to liberty, a right to a fair trial, privacy, freedom of speech etc. The Council of Europe represents a wider group of countries than the EU.

Anyone who believes the law in this country has not dealt fairly with their rights can take their case to the European Court of Human Rights in Strasbourg. The UK has agreed to abide by the findings of the Strasbourg court but this is a long and costly process. Before the *Human Rights Act 1998* came into force the UK courts themselves had no power to deal with human rights cases.

■ BRIEF CASE

In September 1976 Jeffrey, aged 16, took a short cut home from his school in Scotland through a nearby cemetery. This was against school rules and Jeffrey was reported to the head, who decided that he should be punished with the strap. The boy refused. He was supported by his parents; who said that they thought corporal punishment was morally wrong. Jeffrey was suspended.

Both the school and the local authority suggested various ways in which he might be allowed back - but could not promise that Jeffrey would never be beaten for misbehaviour. Jeffrey's parents would not agree to this. They claimed that the local authority were breaking part of the European Convention on Human Rights, which says that no one shall be denied the right to education and that parents have the right to make sure that their children are taught in a way that respects their religious and philosophical beliefs.

When the case eventually reached the European Court of Human Rights in 1982, the Court agreed with Jeffrey's mother, who had made the application. As a result, the British government had to change the law on corporal punishment in schools. This took some time to achieve, but corporal punishment was eventually abolished in most UK schools in 1987.

In 2003 an independent school unsuccessfully challenged this ban in the courts but is appealing.

use the law with care try talking first

The Convention Rights in UK law

There are 16 basic rights in the *Human Rights Act*. They don't only affect matters of life and death like freedom from torture and killing; they also affect people's rights in everyday life: what they can say and do, their beliefs, their right to a fair trial and many other similar basic entitlements.

(Article 1 is introductory)

Article 2 Right to life

Everyone has the absolute right to have their life protected by law. There are only certain very limited circumstances where it is acceptable for the State to take away someone's life, eg if a police officer acts justifiably in self-defence.

Article 3 Prohibition of torture

Everyone has the absolute right not to be tortured or subjected to treatment or punishment that is inhuman or degrading.

Article 4 Prohibition of slavery and forced labour

Everyone has the absolute right not to be treated as a slave or forced to perform certain kinds of labour.

Article 5 Right to liberty and security

Everyone has the right not to be deprived of their liberty – "arrested or detained" - except in limited cases specified in the Article (eg where they are suspected or convicted of committing a crime) and where this is justified by a clear legal procedure.

Human Rights Act 1998

In order to improve access to justice and the fairness of our laws and procedures, the *Human Rights Act 1998* was passed, incorporating into our law nearly all the rights contained in the Convention. Under this Act all our laws must, as far as possible, conform to the rights listed under the Convention, and public bodies – such as the armed forces, local authorities, schools, hospitals, the police, prisons and the courts – must carry out their work in a way that respects these basic human rights. If they don't, then the law or the actions of the public body can be challenged in our own courts. A statute that the courts say is "incompatible" with the rights in the Convention is capable of being changed quickly.

human rights

Article 6 Right to a fair trial

Everyone has the right to a fair and public hearing within a reasonable period of time. This applies to both criminal charges and in sorting out cases concerning civil rights and obligations. Hearings must be by an independent and impartial tribunal established by law. It is possible to exclude the public from the hearing (though not the judgment) in order to protect national security or public order. Anyone who is charged with a criminal charge is presumed innocent until proved guilty according to law and has certain guaranteed rights to defend themselves.

Article 7 No punishment without law

Everyone normally has the right not to be found guilty of an offence arising out of actions which at the time they were committed were not criminal. There is also protection against later increases in the possible sentence for an offence.

Articles 8-11

The rights to the following freedoms (in Articles 8 to 11) may be restricted where this is necessary to protect things like public health or safety, the rights of others or to prevent crime (including racial offences).

Interference with these rights that goes too far can be challenged in the courts who will try to strike a fair balance.

Article 8 Right to respect for private life

Everyone has the right to respect for their private and family life, their home and their correspondence.

Article 9 Freedom of thought, conscience and religion

Everyone is free to hold whatever views, beliefs and thoughts (including religious faith) they like.

Article 10 Freedom of expression

Everyone has the right to express their views on their own or in a group. This applies even if they are unpopular or disturbing. This right can be restricted in specified circumstances.

Article 11 Freedom of assembly and association

Everyone has the right to get together with other people in a peaceful way. They also have the right to associate with other people, which can include the right to form a trade union. These rights may be restricted only in specified circumstances.

Article 12 Right to marry

Men and women have the right to marry and start a family. Our national law still governs how and at what age this can take place.

(Article 13, which deals with legal remedies, is not incorporated into our law)

Article 14 Prohibition of discriminationn

Everyone has the right to benefit from these Convention rights regardless of race, religion, sex, political views or any other status, unless a restriction can be reasonably justified.

HOW DOES THE HUMAN RIGHTS ACT AFFECT US?

The Human Rights Act is a unique type of higher law, affecting all other laws. The rights and their limitations are a set of basic values. Respect for these rights and everything that goes with them may help change the way people think and behave. It should help create a society in which decisions and policies are better discussed and understood. But the freedoms protected by the Act are not a complete set of human values and do not, for example, include the right to work or freedom from poverty.

The Act cannot be used directly by one private individual against another. It is designed to indicate how judges in courts must interpret the law and how public bodies – such as the police, the prison service and local councils – must carry out their actions.

It protects fundamental freedoms – like liberty and free speech – but at the same time, allows limits to be placed on these rights in order to try to make sure that other people are also treated fairly.

For example, a person's right to liberty may be restricted if they are guilty of a serious crime. This is for other people's protection. Similarly there are limits placed on freedom of speech to prevent someone from shouting 'Fire!' in a crowded hall, when there isn't one.

Article 1 of Protocol 1*
Protection of property

Everyone has the right to the peaceful enjoyment of their possessions. Public authorities cannot usually interfere with things we own or the way we use them, except in specified limited circumstances.

Article 2 of Protocol 1*
Right to education

Everyone has the right not to be denied access to the educational system.

Article 3 of Protocol 1*
Right to free elections

Elections must be free and fair, and take place by secret ballot. Some restrictions can be placed on those who are allowed to vote (eg a minimum age).

Articles 1 and 2 of Protocol 6*
Abolition of the death penalty

These provisions abolish the death penalty. There can be limited exceptions in times of war, but only in accordance with clearly specified laws.

* (a 'protocol' is a later addition to the Convention)

voting and elections

Who can vote?

You must be 18 or over on the day of the election and your name must be on the electoral register maintained by your local council. For Parliamentary elections, you must be a citizen of the United Kingdom, the Commonwealth or of the Irish Republic, and live in this country. To vote for the Welsh Assembly you must also be on the electoral register in Wales. For European and local elections, nationals of the EU states living in the UK may also vote.

Who can't vote?

Those unable to vote in Parliamentary elections include most people compulsorily held for treatment for mental illness (although the rights of people in this category are not absolutely clear), most convicted prisoners, anyone convicted of corrupt practices at an election during the previous five years and members of the House of Lords.

Registering to vote

You can register to vote at any time by contacting your local council election registration office. An electoral registration form is also delivered to every household in the country. The form should be completed with details of everyone living there, aged 16 and over. Registering to vote is not linked in any way to paying taxes, but it is technically an offence knowingly to fail to put yourself on the electoral register.

Anyone can get a postal vote, provided that they are on the electoral register. There are also special arrangements for people who cannot get to the polling station on the day.

Experiments to make the process of voting more up-to-date include mobile polling stations and "e-voting" through the Internet, mobile phones and digital TV.

You can check if your name is on the register of electors at your local main library or council offices.

use the law with care **try talking first**

Who can you vote for?

Most people who want to be elected as an MP, MEP, AM or local Councillor represent a political party. All political parties have to be registered with the Electoral Commission. The party will then select its candidates for each election. Some people stand as an independent without belonging to any political party.

Local elections

The election of local councillors is held every four years, usually in the first week of May, although not all councils hold them in the same year.

Between them, and sometimes together with national government, these councils are responsible for education, planning, refuse, environment, recreation, passenger transport, libraries, social services, children's homes, council housing and car parks.

As well as deciding how the services are to be run, local councillors also take up problems on behalf of those living in their area.

LOCAL COUNCILLOR, AM, MP OR MEP?

You can stand for political office from the age of 21. If you want to be a local councillor you must either...

- have your name on the local electoral register; or
- rent or own land or property or
- have worked in the area for the last twelve months; or
- have lived in, or within three miles of, the area for the last twelve months.

These rules do not apply to Welsh Assembly members, MPs or MEPs. Candidates standing as an AM or MP must pay a deposit of £500, which they lose if they get less than 5% of the votes cast. The deposit for MEPs is £5,000.

General elections

The election of 659 MPs must take place at least every five years. Often, however, the party in power will call an election before this if it feels it will help its chances of gaining another term of office, or more rarely, because it has been defeated on a vital vote in the House of Commons and has lost the confidence of the House.

Most MPs represent a registered political party and each represents a defined area, called a constituency. The party with the greatest number of MPs forms the government, with the party leader becoming Prime Minister. If an MP dies or resigns, a by-election takes place to elect a new MP for the constituency.

Even if not a member of the Government, an MP can have influence by speaking in debates, talking to ministers and other MPs, and by trying to get a private member's Bill made law. MPs must represent everyone in their constituency.

Voting systems

Votes for general and by-elections in the United Kingdom are counted on a 'first past the post' system. People each cast one vote and the winning candidate is the one with the most votes. Elections to the Assembly for Wales and the European Parliament follow a different system called proportional representation. Under this system, the number of seats that each party receives is roughly equal to their share of the votes. There is the possibility that the voting system for MPs will be changed to one of proportional representation. The Government has said that it plans to hold a vote or referendum on this.

European elections

At European elections we elect members of the European Parliament that meets both in Strasbourg (France) and Brussels (Belgium). They take place every five years. Most candidates belong to one of the main political parties and, if elected, join the MEPs of the 14 other countries in the European Union. The UK has 87 MEPs (out of a current total of 626). MEPs sit in multinational political groups so for example, British Labour MEPs belong to the Party of European Socialists, along with socialists from the other EU states.

MEPs help to make European law by examining and commenting on proposals made by the European Commission (see **europe** pages 132-133).

Campaigning

If you feel strongly about something and want to get involved yourself, a library, Citizens Advice Bureau, or one of the organisations or websites listed in the **contacts** section can probably give you some of the information you need to find out who to contact.

This ranges from individual action to something more co-ordinated, as a member of a group. Letter writing is the usual starting point - do your research, send it to a named person (the most senior within the organisation), keep a copy, and try to get others involved as well. If you can get a letter published in a newspaper, many more will know about your views, but do give your name and address - although you can ask the paper not to publish it.

Writing to your councillor, MP or MEP

If your problem is local, contact your local councillor through the council office. AMs, MPs or MEPs can best take up problems for which the Government or European Union are responsible. Most AMs, MPs and some MEPs have local 'surgeries' for which no appointment is necessary. They are often held on a Saturday, and advertised in the local paper. You can also write to your AM or MEP locally and your MP at the House of Commons. Addresses are obtainable from the local library, and are listed under Member of Parliament in the business section of the phone book. Some MPs also have their own websites.

Protest

The same laws apply to people taking part in political action as any other area of life. Criminal damage, theft, assault etc. remain crimes - no matter how good the cause.

Demonstrations and marches are controlled by the *Public Order Act 1986* and the *Criminal Justice and Public Order Act 1994*. Organisers must inform the local police where and when the march will take place and how many people will be involved. If the police believe the demonstration is likely to disrupt seriously the life of the community, a senior police officer can issue a ban for a period of up to three months.

Trespassing

The *Criminal Justice and Public Order Act 1994* introduced the offence of aggravated trespass. It was aimed at hunt saboteurs, but can affect anyone who causes disruption to people going about their lawful business. It is an offence to trespass on private land in order to intimidate, obstruct or disrupt people (such as trying to distract the hounds by blowing horns), who are doing a lawful activity.

Complaining

If you have a complaint about something you have bought or a service you have received, it's important to act quickly. Some companies, and many public services, have special procedures for dealing with complaints. If it's a public service, such as a hospital or benefits agency, you can ask to see a copy of their charter which shows the level of service you are entitled to expect. If your complaint is not dealt with properly, think about contacting your local councillor or MP, particularly if your problem is over a public service.

- act as quickly as possible,
- think carefully about what you want to achieve and if necessary get advice;
- make sure you talk or write directly to a person - such as the manager or director of services - who has the authority to deal with your complaint;
- always find out the name of the person you are talking to;
- keep a record of phone calls or letters that you send;
- stick to the facts, and work out how the law can help you;
- state clearly what you want to be done, set a reasonable time within which this should happen, and get back in touch if they haven't met the deadline.

If you are still unhappy with the way your problem has been handled, you may be able to take your case to an Ombudsman. See **contacts**, General.

Judicial review

If a public body - like a government department, local authority, or hospital - makes a decision which actually seems to be fundamentally unfair , you can apply to have that decision reviewed in the High Court. Known as judicial review, it's a way of having illegal or unreasonable decisions changed. Examples of this have been when people have challenged a ruling by the Home Office to deport someone who is a British citizen, or when they have questioned a hospital's right to withhold an operation in a genuinely urgent case.

A judicial review can normally be started only when all other avenues of complaint have been exhausted. It's a very complicated and expensive process and so, before doing anything, it's important to get advice from a solicitor who understands this area of law.

the european union

young citizen's **passport**

INDIVIDUALS ENGAGING IN SOCIETY

Citizenship Foundation

Fifteen countries are currently members of the European Union (EU) .

Austria, Belgium, Denmark, Finland, France, Germany, Greece, Ireland, Italy, Luxembourg, the Netherlands, Portugal, Spain, Sweden, and the United Kingdom.

Ten more states join the EU on 1 May 2004: Cyprus, the Czech Republic, Estonia, Hungary, Latvia, Lithuania, Malta, Poland, Slovakia, and Slovenia . Bulgaria and Romania are likely to join in 2007, and it is expected that negotiations will also begin with Turkey.

Origins

After the end of the Second World War, governments throughout Europe were determined not to repeat the horrors of the War, in which 50 million people had died.

From 1945, European states began increasingly to co-operate with one another in many different ways. One of the most important things that this produced is the European Union (EU) - an organisation of member states, with a total population of more than 370 million people.

In the early years co-operation was mainly designed to make it easier for member states to trade with one another. Gradually, the scope of the union has widened, and covers many areas today, including employment, the environment, transport, travel, foreign policy – and for twelve of the member states a common currency – the euro.

The idea of European states forming a single market has always been central to the development of the European Union.

A single market means that goods, services, people, and money must be able to move freely between member states.

Over the last 30 years member states have agreed all kinds of measures to make this possible:

- **taxes and duties on products have been made broadly similar between member states,**
- **technical and safety specifications of goods have been standardised, so that goods made in one state meet the standards required in another,**
- **people are allowed to travel, live, study, and work more-or-less wherever they wish.**

A single currency

The EU has also eased the movement of goods and people through the creation of a single currency, also sometimes called economic and monetary union (EMU)

The idea was first proposed in 1969, but the first significant steps were not taken until around 1990 when member states interested in moving towards a single currency began to prepare their economies for this process.

They were required to meet a number of conditions – usually described as convergence criteria – such as having low interest rates, keeping currency rates and prices stable and keeping government expenditure within certain limits.

The Euro

On 1st January 2002, after a transition period of two years, twelve of the fifteen EU member states moved to a single currency – the euro (€).

Since 28th February 2002, euro banknotes and coins have been the sole legal tender within these 12 countries.

The seven euro notes, from €5 - €500 are the same throughout the single currency area. Each country produces its own coins, of smaller value, although these can be used anywhere within the euro area, regardless of national origin.

Britain and the Euro

Britain, Denmark, and Sweden decided not to proceed with the single currency. Denmark has held two national referendums on joining the euro, rejecting the idea on both occasions. In 2003, the people of Sweden voted against the euro. The British government has also undertaken to hold a referendum on the issue when the government believes that its own five convergence criteria have been met.

Measures have been gradually introduced to help people move around the EU as easily as possible.

Travel

Citizens of an EU member state have the right to travel to any EU country, if they have a valid passport or identity card. This right may be restricted only for reasons of public order, public security, or public health.

EU citizens also have the right to travel within the EU with members of their family, but if they do not have EU nationality they may be required to have a visa, in addition to their passport.

Border controls There are no customs checks for people travelling from one EU member state to another – although police controls on some frontiers remain, checking for terrorist activity, drug-trafficking and organised crime.

In addition, identity checks for EU citizens, have been abolished at many borders under what is called the Schengen Agreement. This allows people to travel from one country to another without having their passport or identity documents examined. All member states except Britain and Ireland have joined this group.

Health care

Citizens of EU member states who fall ill within another EU country are entitled to emergency treatment under that country's health scheme.

The treatment is free to someone from Britain who can show the medical authorities form E111, available from UK

social security or main post offices.

A person who doesn't have an E111 is still entitled to treatment but may be asked to pay its full cost.

Help An EU citizen who gets into difficulties in a country outside the EU may seek protection from the embassy or consulate of any EU member state.

For example, a British student arrested in a Russian city without a British consular office is entitled to help from the Swedish or Finnish consulate.

Work

British citizens are entitled to work in any EU country, and should be offered employment under the same conditions as citizens of that state. It would be against the law, for example, for an Italian firm to require British job applicants to have higher qualifications than their Italian counterparts – and vice versa.

Most jobs are open to all EU citizens. However, member states are allowed to insist that only nationals of that state hold certain public service posts, such as those in the police or armed forces. A residence permit is required for anyone who wants to stay in another member state for more than three months. This requires ID and evidence of financial support.

Conditions

Generally speaking, a British citizen working in an EU member state has exactly the same employment rights and duties as everyone else in that country, and it is against the law for that person to be discriminated against on grounds of their nationality.

A British worker in Berlin, for example, should receive the same pay, employment opportunities, and health and safety protection as his or her German counterparts.

Qualifications

The EU operates on the system that someone qualified to work in a particular profession in their own country is also able to carry out that work in any other member state. However not all qualifications are automatically recognised – although applicants are able to check if their particular diploma or certificate is recognised.

Benefits

Citizens of EU member states are entitled to the same welfare and social security benefits as nationals of the country where they are working. This covers sickness and maternity benefits, benefits for accidents at work and unemployment. They also have the same rights, where it is available, to accommodation, such as local authority housing.

Taxes

A person who lives and works in an EU member state must normally pay taxes in the same way as any other resident of that country. Levels of taxation vary from one EU state to another.

goods

Customs duties

Generally speaking, goods purchased by people for their own use may be bought in other member states and brought back to Britain without having to pay extra tax or duties. The few exceptions include new cars, boats, and aeroplanes.

People can bring in as much tobacco and alcohol as they like, if the items were bought in the EU and can show that they are for personal use only and not for resale. Customs officials in the UK have the right to stop people and check this, confiscating any items they believe are not for personal use.

The structure of the government of the European Union is not easy to understand - possibly because there are several organisations that help to determine EU policy.

THE EUROPEAN COUNCIL

The European Council is the name given to the regular meetings between the heads of the member states. They decide the issues the European Union should be concerned with. In the past this has included unemployment, drug trafficking, and enlarging the EU.

The Council of Ministers

The Council of Ministers is one of the most influential bodies in the EU. It consists of government ministers from each member state with powers to adopt new laws, take decisions about how the EU is run, recommend policy, and negotiate with non-member states on behalf of the EU. It's at the centre government in the EU, rather like the Cabinet is in Britain.

Decisions Until the mid 1980s, decisions by the Council of Ministers tended to have to be unanimous. If a nation disagreed, the measure could not be passed. Today the Council generally uses a system called qualified majority voting. Each member state has a certain number of votes, broadly reflecting the size of the country in terms of its population.

France, Germany, Italy, and the United Kingdom have 10 votes. Smaller countries, like Finland and Ireland have 3. 62 votes are required to pass a new law.

However, this system of voting will change when the EU expands in 2004.

The European Commission

Based in Brussels, the European Commission is rather like the civil service of the European Union, taking care of the day-to-day running of the organisation. Almost 30,000 people work for the Commission, making it one of Europe's largest institutions.

The Commission does several different jobs. It:

- **drafts proposals for new EU laws or policies,**
- **checks that EU laws and treaties are properly applied,**
- **begins legal action against member states or businesses that it believes are not following EU law.**

EU Commissioners Each member state appoints one or two commissioners to take responsibility for running one particular aspect of EU business.

There are currently 20 Commissioners in all. The President, appointed from 2000-2005, is Romano Prodi, from Italy. Neil Kinnock, former leader of the Labour Party, is vice-president. The other British Commissioner is Chris Patten, a former Conservative minister, who is responsible for links between the EU and other states. From November 2004 each country will nominate one Commissioner.

The European Parliament

The European Parliament currently consists of 626 MEPs (Members of the European Parliament). However this will rise to 732 seats after enlargement in 2004. The Parliament meets in Brussels, Luxembourg and Strasbourg.

In the course of a month, MEPs usually meet for one week in Strasbourg, and for two weeks, on committee work, in Brussels. Parliamentary support staff are based in Brussels and Luxembourg.

Powers

Today, MEPs:
- **decide, together with the Council of Ministers, on EU law,**
- **control more than half the money that the EU spends,**
- **watch over the European Commission and approve the appointment of all Commissioners.**

Elections

The UK is allocated 87 of the 626 seats in the European Parliament. From June 2004 the UK will have 78 of the 732 seats. At the last election in 1999, the Conservatives became the largest UK party in the European Parliament. The turnout in 1999 was lower than in previous years, particularly in the UK.

Voting

In the UK, as in any other EU member state, voting in European Parliamentary elections is open to any EU citizen, provided they are on the local register of electors.

Contact

Debates in the European Parliament are open to the public, and groups and individuals can visit the Parliamentary building. MEPs may be reached by e-mail or by post or phone at their constituency office.

Petitions

All EU citizens have the right to submit a petition to the President of the European Parliament (the address is L - 2929 Luxembourg) giving their view on a matter that is within the remit of the EU. The petition can be in any form – as long as it contains the sender's name, address, occupation, and signature.

■ BRIEF CASE

In 1999, the European Parliament ordered an investigation into fraud and corruption by members of the European Commission. The report of the investigation was very critical of the Commission and led to all 20 Commissioners resigning.

■ BRIEF CASE

Following a recent successful petition to the EU, the Greek authorities are now required to admit EU citizens to their museums under the same conditions as Greek nationals.

Today in Britain, MPs and judges still create and shape the law in much the same way as they have done for several hundred years. See pages 114-115.

However our membership of the European Union requires all our laws to follow the treaties and agreements that we have made as members of the EU.

In this sense European law has become the most important source of law in Britain. This is not to say that all our law comes from Europe, but it does mean that all our current and future laws must not break the principles set out in the treaties that we have signed.

■ BRIEF CASE: Patricia

In 1994, British courts heard the case of Patricia Day who was made redundant after working for nearly five years as a part-time cleaner. Her employer, Hertfordshire County Council, stated that under UK law she was not entitled to any redundancy pay because she worked for less than 16 hours a week.

The judges decided that, although this practice did not break UK law it was a form of discrimination against women, as most of the part-time workforce was female.

As sex discrimination in employment was expressly forbidden in European Union law, the British government had to change the law. Shortly afterwards the law was altered to give full and part-time workers similar employment rights.

The European Union

Law created through our membership of the European Union normally reaches us in four ways – through treaties, regulations, directives, and court judgements.

Treaties

Treaties are agreements made between our government and other EU member states, which become incorporated into our law by Parliament. Treaties often contain broad agreements on which further action will be based. Sometimes, however, they include sections that can have a very specific effect on people's lives.

■ BRIEF CASE

The Treaty of Rome, signed in 1957, is the agreement upon which the European Economic Community was established. Article 119 of the Treaty states that men and women should receive equal pay for equal work.

Regulations Regulations are the laws that put treaties into practice.

Directives Directives, like regulations, are a means of putting an EU objective into practice, but member states are able to choose for themselves how this will be done.

■ BRIEF CASE

An important section of the Treaty of Rome says that people should be able to move freely for work between member states. The regulations that have followed the Treaty require member states to introduce new laws to ensure this works. As a result, all member states needed to have laws granting visiting EU workers the same rights to education and housing as the citizens of their own state.

■ BRIEF CASE

In 2001, the EU issued a directive requiring companies operating in the EU to inform employees about any decision affecting their jobs – especially if it might lead to redundancy. This directive was made following a number of unexpected redundancies in France, issued by several multi-national companies. The UK was given seven years in which to implement the directive.

Court judgements The European Court of Justice considers all matters of European Community law. Located in Luxembourg, it is the most senior court in Europe and overrules all national courts. Member states must follow its decisions.

■ BRIEF CASE: John

Until recently, UK winter fuel payments were paid to women from the age 60, but not to men until they reached 65. This was challenged in the UK courts by retired postman John Taylor, who claimed it was unlawful discrimination. The British High Court asked the European Court of Justice to deliver a judgement on this in the light of European Community law. The European Court announced that this practice did not follow community law and that winter fuel payments should be given to men and women under the same terms.

• **Before you write, phone or ask for information,** think carefully about exactly what you need to know. Don't be overlong in your explanation, keep to the most important details.

• **If you are telephoning, you will** probably first speak to a receptionist who may not be able to answer your question. Explain that you'd like to talk to someone about…(name the subject), and you should be put through. If they can't help, they may be able to give you the name of someone who can.

• **It sometimes helps to put a few** key words down on paper to remind you of what you want to say. You may also need a pen and paper to make a note of what you are told.

• **It's a good idea to ask who you** are talking to so, if you write or phone again, you know the name of the person you first spoke to.

The following names and details are arranged according to the chapters in the main part of the book and are just a few of the many organisations that can help with the whole range of law-related problems.

General

Childline, Freepost NATN 1111, London E1 6BR. A free 24hr helpline for any child in danger or distress, tel 0800 1111. **www.childline.org.uk**

Children's Legal Centre, University of Essex, Wivenhoe Park, Colchester, Essex CO4 3SQ, offers advice on a wide range of issues by letter and phone. The advice line is open Mon-Fri 10-12.30, tel 01206 873 820. **www.childrenslegalcentre.com**

Citizens Advice Bureau, or CAB, gives free, confidential and independent information and advice on all kinds of problems. You can enquire by phone or at one of their offices in most towns and cities. For your nearest CAB, see the local phone book, **www.nacab.org.uk** and for advice **www.adviceguide.org.uk**

Community Legal Service, government information on legal services for the community: tel 0845 608 1122. Their web site Just Ask! will help locate legal advice in your area and find legal information on carefully selected web sites: **www.justask.org.gov**

Disability Law Services, Ground Floor, 39-45 Cavell Street, London E1 2BP, tel 020 7791 9800/9821; email: advice@dls.org.uk. Free legal advice for disabled people on benefits, education, employment, consumer issues, children and community care.

Free Representation Unit, Room 140,1st Floor,49/51 Bedford Row London WC1X 8LZ. A network of barristers and law students who will represent clients without charge at social security and employment tribunals. They only take cases referred to them by solicitors, law centres and CABs. Please do not call directly.

Information Shops, are specifically designed for young people and organised by the **National Youth Agency**, with trained workers able to provide information and support. For details of your nearest Information Shop, contact the National Youth Agency, 17-23 Albion Street, Leicester LE1 6GD, tel 0116 285 3700, email: nya@nya.org.uk, **www.nya.org.uk**

Law Centres Federation, Duchess House, 18-19 Warren Street, London W1T 5LR, tel 020 7387 8570, email: info@lawcentres.org.uk, can give you the name and address of your nearest Law Centre where free or low cost legal advice on a range of topics can be obtained. **www.lawcentres.org.uk**

Law Society, 113 Chancery Lane, London WC2A 1PL, tel 020 7242 1222, email: enquiries@lawsociety.org.uk, provides information on using a solicitor. **www.lawsociety.org.uk.** To make a complaint about a solicitor, contact the **Office for the Supervision of Solicitors**, Victoria Ct., 8 Dormer Place, Leamington Spa, Warwickshire, CV32 5AE, tel 01926 820082. **www.oss.lawsociety.org.uk**

Liberty, 21 Tabard Street, London SE1 4LA, tel 020 7403 3888. A campaigning organisation able to answer questions from people who feel their civil liberties have been infringed. A legal advice line is open on Mon and Thurs 6-8pm, Wed 12.30-2.30pm, tel 020 7378 8659. **www.liberty-human-rights.org.uk**

The Ombudsman. If you have a problem with your local authority, a government department, the health service, an insurance company, a bank or building society or a legal service, and are not happy with how your complaint has been dealt with, you can refer your case to the relevant Ombudsman. You must first, however, have done everything you can to sort things out yourself with the person or organisation concerned. Your local CAB can explain how to submit a complaint, or you can contact the appropriate office at one of the addresses below. If the Ombudsman decides your complaint is reasonable, the department or organisation responsible will be asked to do something about it - which might mean that you get an apology or compensation. New procedures may also be put into place to make sure the same thing doesn't happen again.

The Local Government Ombudsman (for England), 10th Floor, Millbank Tower, Millbank, London SW1P4QP, tel 0207 217 4620, advice line 9-4.30 Mon- Fri 0845 602 1983, **www.lgo.org.uk,** and (for Wales), Derwen House, Court Road, Bridgend CF31 1BN, tel 01656 661325, **www.ombudsman-wales.org.uk**; the **Parliamentary Ombudsman**, tel 0845 015 4033; the **Health Service Ombudsman**, 11th Floor, Millbank Tower, London SW1P

4QP, **www.ombudsman.org.uk**; and (for Wales), 5th Floor, Capital Tower, Greyfriars Road, Cardiff CF1 3AG, tel 0845 600987; **The Financial Ombudsman Service**, South Quay Plaza,183 Marsh Wall, London E14 9SR, **www.obo.org.uk**; the **Office of Legal Service Ombudsman**, 3rd Floor, Sunlight House, Quay Street, Manchester M3 3JZ, tel 0845 601 0794, **www.olso.org**

Solicitors give advice on legal problems, take action for you on your behalf and represent you in many courts or tribunals (they may engage a barrister to appear in higher courts).

There are solicitors' offices in every town and city in England and Wales. Many solicitors take publicly funded or conditional fee cases, and some will give you a free introductory interview. However when you first make contact, it's important to ask how much the work will cost. Choosing the right firm of solicitors is important. The Law Society, the Just Ask! website or your local CAB can give you the name of firms specialising in cases involving your particular problem.

Youth Access, 1-2 Taylor's Yard, 67 Alderbrook Road, London SW12 8AD, tel 020 8772 9900, email: admin@youthaccess.org.uk If you have a problem of any kind you would like to discuss confidentially, Youth Access can put you in touch with someone locally who may be able to help. There is no charge for their service. **www.youthaccess.org.uk**

| Life | SEX, CONTRACEPTION, PREGNANCY AND ABORTION |

AFLaGA (formerly Rank Outsiders), BCM Box 8431, London WC1N 3XX, can give advice and support to serving and ex-serving members of the armed forces who are lesbian or gay. The helpline, tel 0870 740 7755, operates Wed 7-9pm & Sun 9am-7pm, but messages can also be left outside this time. **www.aflaga.org.uk**

British Agencies for Adoption and Fostering, Skyline House, 200 Union Street, London SE1 0LX, tel 020 7593 2000 offer advice and information on adoption and fostering and can put you in touch with an office near you. **www.baaf.org.uk**

British Pregnancy and Advisory Service, has over 40 centres nationwide able to provide pregnancy tests, consultation and emergency contraception, and to undertake abortions. For BPA's Actionline tel 0845 7 30 40 30. **www.bpas.org**

Brook Advisory Centres, offer free and confidential advice and counselling on sex and contraception for young people under 25, covering the whole of the UK. An advice line is open Mon- Fri 9am-5 pm, tel 0800 0185 023. **www.brook.org.uk**; 24 hour recorded info, tel 020 767 8000.

fpa, 2-12 Pentonville Road, London N1 9FP tel 020 7837 5432 runs a contraceptive education helpline, Mon-Fri 9am-7pm, tel 0845 310 1334, **www.fpa.org.uk**; and for Wales, **fpa** Cymru, Suite D, Canton House, 435-451 Cambridge Road East, Cardiff CF5 1JH, tel 029 2064 4034 - can give addresses of local family planning clinics and answer questions about contraception and reproductive health. There is a second office in Bangor, tel 01248 353 534.

Gay and Lesbian Legal Advice, (GLAD), 16 Clerkenwell Close, London EC1R 0AA, offers legal advice and assistance to lesbians and gay men, open Mon-Thurs, 7-9.30pm.

Maternity Alliance, 2-6 Northburgh St, London EC1V 0AY run an advice line for pregnant women and new parents, open Mon, Tues, Thurs & Fri, 10.30am-12.30pm, tel 020 7490 7638, email: info@maternityalliance.org.uk. Able to provide information on a wide range of issues, including antenatal care, employment rights and benefits for pregnant women. **www.maternityalliance.org.uk**

Sexual Health Wales, can also provide lists of agencies 8am-8pm weekdays and 10am- 2pm weekends on 0845 604 8484.

Stonewall, 46-48 Grosvenor Gardens, London SW1W 0EB, tel 020 7881 9440, email:info@stonewall.org.uk, campaigns for equality for lesbians, gay men and bisexuals and can provide information on these issues. **www.stonewall.org.uk**

HIV and AIDS

The 1990 Trust website **www.blink.org.uk** links to **www.healthweb.blink.org.uk**, which provides information for people of African, Asian and Caribbean extraction on a variety of health issues including HIV/AIDS.

National AIDS Helpline, a 24hr freephone service, staffed by advisors who can deal with questions on sex, drugs or relationships, tel 0800 567 123. A Welsh language option available.

NAZ Project London, Palingswick House, 241 King Street, London W6 9LP, tel 020 8741 1879. email: naz@naz.org.uk. Advice and support on HIV, AIDS and sexual health for people from S Asian, Middle Eastern, N African, Latin American & Horn of Africa communities. **www.naz.org.uk.**

Positively Women, practical and emotional support for women with HIV and AIDS. 347-349 City Road, London EC1V 1LR, tel 020 7713 0444, helpline 020 7713 1020. 10am-4pm Mon-Fri. **www.positivelywomen.org.uk**

Terrence Higgins Trust, 52-54 Gray's Inn Road, London WC1X 8JU, tel 020 7242 1010, 7 days a week, 12noon-10pm, and **London Lighthouse**, 111-117 Lancaster Road, London W11 1QT, tel 020 7792 1200 and the THT Direct helpline, tel 0845 1221 200, Mon-Fri 10am-10pm, Sat-Sun 12noon-6pm, provides support and information for people affected with HIV and AIDS. **www.tht.org.uk**

use the law with care **try talking first**

DRUGS AND ADDICTION

Drugaid (Wales), MIDAS 2nd Floor, Oldway House, Castle St, Merthyr Tydfil, Mid Glamorgan, CD47 8UX, tel 01685 721991, 16 Clive St, Caerphilly, Mid Glamorgan, CF83 1JQ, tel 029 2088 1000, and 1A Bartlett St,Caerphilly, CF83 1 JS, offering counselling, support and information for drug and alcohol users, their friends and family. **www.drugaidcymru.com**

DrugScope, 32-36 Loman Street, London SE1 0EE, tel 020 7928 1211. Information about drug advice agencies in your area. **www.drugscope.org.uk**

FRANK (formerly the National Drugs Helpline) , a 24hr free confidential helpline providing advice and information on all types of drug taking for drug users, their family and friends, tel 0800 77 66 00, (a Welsh language service is available between 11am-11pm), email: frank@talktofrank.com. **www.talktofrank.com**

Narcotics Anonymous, tel 020 7730 0009, a confidential helpline, open 10am-10pm, 7 days a week, for those trying to recover from addiction. **www.ukna.org**

Release, 388 Old Street, London EC1V 9LT; information and legal advice service on drug-related problems, Mon-Fri, 10am-6pm, tel 020 7729 5255, email: info@ release.org.uk Provides legal advice and heroin helpline. Overnight & weekend helpline, tel 020 7603 8654. **www.release.org.uk**

HEALTH

Community Health Councils in Wales give advice to anyone who feels they have a complaint about any aspect of the health services. Under 'C' in the phone book.

MIND, Granta House, 15-19 Broadway, London E15 4BQ, tel 020 8519 2122, email:contact@mind.org.uk. Information on all aspects of mental health. Infoline: 0845 766 0163. **www.mind.org.uk**

NHS Direct, a 24hr helpline providing confidential advice to anyone concerned about their health, or with questions about any aspect of the Health Service, tel 0845 4647. **www.nhsdirect.nhs.uk**

Samaritans, will talk to anyone feeling desperate, lonely or suicidal. You can say what you like, you need not give your name, it's entirely confidential. They can be reached by phone at any time, every day of the year. The central number is 0847 90 90 90 or, for your local branch, look under 'S' in the phone book. **www.samaritans.org.uk**

Sane, 1st Floor, Cityside House, 40 Adler Street, London E1 1EE, tel 020 7375 1002, able to provide information and advice to anyone (including friends and family) suffering mental health problems. They can also give callers the names of solicitors prepared to give up to an hour's free advice and put them in touch with support available in their local area. A helpline operates every day of the year between 12noon-2am, tel 0845 767 8000. **www.sane.org.uk**

Safety

PERSONAL SAFETY

Commission for Racial Equality, St Dunstans House, 201-211 Borough High Street, London SE1 1GZ, tel 020 7939 0000, can give information on the law relating to racial harassment and the phone number of your local racial equality council. **www.cre.gov.uk**

Kidscape, 2 Grosvenor Gardens, London SW1W 0DH, tel 020 7730 3300, provides free information and advice on keeping safe, including bullying and how to cope with it, open Mon-Fri 10am-4pm. **www.kidscape.org.uk**

Rape Crisis Federation England and Wales, Unit 7 Provident Works, Newdigate St, Nottingham, NG7 4FD runs Rape Crisis Centres, located throughout Britain offering free and confidential advice to any woman or girl who has been raped or sexually assaulted. Tel 0115 900 3560, email: info@rapecrisis.co.uk for details of your local centre. **www.rapecrisis.co.uk**

Survivors, PO Box 2470, London SW9 9ZP, tel 020 7613 0808, email: info@survivorsuk.org.uk. A helpline is open Mon-Tues 7-10pm, giving advice and information to men who are victims of sexual violence. **www.survivorsuk.co.uk**

Suzy Lamplugh Trust, 14 East Sheen Avenue, London SW14 8WW, tel 020 8392 1839, email: trust@suzylamplugh.org. Practical information, guidance and resources on personal safety in all situations. **www.suzylamplugh.org**

VICTIMS AND COMPENSATION

The **Court Service** publishes the Courts' Charter and other information for victims of crime, available from The Customer Service Unit, The Court Service, Southside, 105 Victoria Street, London SW1E 6QT, tel 020 7210 2266/2269, email: cust.ser.cs@gfnet.gov.uk. Copies of the Victim's Charter are available from libraries and the Home Office, tel 020 7273 2066. **www.courtservice.gov.uk**

Criminal Injuries Compensation Authority, Morley House, 26-30 Holborn Viaduct, London EC1A 2JQ, tel 020 7842 6800 and Tay House, 300 Bath Street, Glasgow, G2 4JN, tel 0141 331 2726, provides compensation for victims of crimes of violence. Write or phone for information and application forms. **www.cica.gov.uk**

Victim Support, Cranmer House, 39 Brixton Road, London SW9 6DZ, tel 020 7735 9166. There is a helpline providing support to people who have been victims of crime, Mon-Fri 9am-9pm and Sat-Sun 9am-7pm, tel 0845 30 30 900. **www.victimsupport.com**

Education

The Advisory Centre for Education (ACE), Unit 1c Aberdeen Studios, 22 Highbury Grove, London N5 2DQ, offers telephone advice, Mon-Fri 2-5pm, tel 0808 800 5793 (free) or 020 7704 9822, email: enquiries@ace.dialnet.com, for questions about exclusions. **www.ace-ed.org.uk**

Department for Education and Skills, Public Enquiry Unit, tel 0870 000 2288, provides information and answer questions about the law relating to education. **www.dfes.gov.uk**

Education Otherwise, PO Box 7420, London N9 9SG, provides information and advice for people choosing to educate their children out of school, tel 0870 730 0074, email: enquiries@education-otherwise.org **www.education-otherwise.org**

Independent Schools Information Service, Grosvenor Gardens House,35-37 Grosvenor Gardens,London SW1W 0BS, London, SW1E 6AG, tel 020 7798 1500, email: info@isis.uk.net, for information on education in the independent sector. **www.isis.org.uk**

use the law with care **try talking first**

Work and Training

Commission for Racial Equality, St Dunstan's House, 201-211 Borough High St, London SE1 1GZ, tel 020 7939 0000, email: info@cre.gov.uk. Information on all aspects of the Race Relations Acts, including problems with employment, housing, harassment and unfair discrimination. **www.cre.gov.uk**

Department for Education and Skills, Public Enquiry Unit, tel 0870 000 2288, for information on the law relating to both training and disabilities. **www.dfes.gov.uk**

Department of Trade and Industry, tel 020 7215 5000, for information on employment law. **www.dti.gov.uk.** For maternity pay **www.tiger.gov.uk**

Equal Opportunities Commission, Arndale House, Arndale Centre, Manchester M4 3EQ, tel 0161 838 1733 and Windsor House, Windsor Lane, Cardiff CF10 3GE, tel 029 2064 1079, for information on a wide range of sex discrimination and gender issues. The Information Section is open Mon-Fri 9.30am-4.30pm. Helpline 08456 015901. **www.eoc.org.uk**

Health and Safety Executive Information Services, Caerphilly Business Park, Caerphilly CF83 3GG. The Health & Safety Executive are responsible for checking health and safety at work throughout England and Wales. They can send information explaining the law and can tell you who to contact if you have a health and safety problem. They also run the HSE Infoline, tel 0870 154 5500, open Mon-Fri 8.00-6.00. **www.hse.gov.uk**

Lesbian and Gay Employment Rights (LAGER), Unit 1g, Leroy House, 436 Essex Road, London N1 3QP, tel 020 7704 2205 advising lesbians and gay men encountering discrimination at work because of their sexuality, tel 020 7704 8066 (lesbian rights) and 020 7704 6066 (gay men). **www.lager.dircon.co.uk**

Maternity Alliance, 2-6 Northburgh St, London EC1V0AY. A 24 hour recorded advice line for pregnant women and new parents, tel 020 7490 7368. Information on the rights and benefits for pregnant women. See also under Life. **www.maternityalliance.org.uk**

Money

Association of British Insurers, Consumer Information Dept., 51 Gresham Street, London EC2V 7HQ, tel 020 7600 3333, for leaflets and further information on insurance. **www.abi.org.uk**

Benefits, administered by the Department for Work and Pensions. For information on benefits, contact your local Jobcentre Plus or Social Security office listed in the phone book. The Disability and Carers service runs a free Benefit Enquiry Line for carers or people with an illness or disability, tel 0800 88 22 00. **www.dwp.gov.uk** and **www.jobcentreplus.gov.uk**

Inland Revenue, free information leaflets on taxation and general enquiries are available from PO Box 37, St Austell, Cornwall, PL25 5YN or from any Inland Revenue enquiry centre. Details from **www.inlandrevenue.gov.uk**

National Debtline, 0808 8084000 (free), for confidential help with debt problems and advice packs. email: advice@nationaldebtline.co.uk. **www.nationaldebtline.co.uk**

Office of Fair Trading, Fleetbank House, 2-6 Salisbury Square, London EC4Y 8JX. The official watchdog, protecting consumers' interests. They can't give advice on individual cases, but can send information on the law or put you in touch with someone who may be able to help. The Public Liaison Unit, tel 08457 22 44 99, can refer general enquiries and consumer complaints. **www.oft.gov.uk**

Trading Standards Offices, are in almost every town and city and give free advice on a wide range of consumer problems. The address of your local office will be in the phone book, under 'T', or available from your local county or borough council or from **www.tradingstandards.gov.uk**

Family

Adoption Contact Register, Office for National Statistics, General Register Office, Adoptions Section, Trafalgar Road, Birkdale, Southport PR8 2HH, tel 0151 471 4830. for adopted people and their birth relatives, who wish to get in touch by the Internet. **www.ukbirth-adoptionregister.com.**

British Association for Adoption and Fostering (BAAF), tel 0207 593 2000 provides advice and information for those thinking of adopting or fostering. **www.BAAF.org.uk.**

Childline, free 24hr. helpline for any child in danger and distress, tel 0800 1111. For counselling centres throughout the UK ,Text phone 0800 400 222. **www.childline.org.uk**

Kidscape, 2 Grosvenor Gardens, London SW1W 0DH, tel 020 7730 3300, provides free information and advice on keeping safe, including bullying and how to cope with it, open Mon-Fri 9am-4pm. **www.kidscape.org.uk**

Law Society Children Panel, The Law Society, Ipsley Court, Berrington Close, Redditch, Worcestershire B98 0TD, tel 01527 517141, can put you in touch with a local solicitor who can advise and represent you in matters concerning parental and other family relationships. **www.lawsociety.org.uk**

Message Home Helpline, a confidential service allowing someone who has run away from home to leave a message for family and friends to let them know they are alive and well and can make referrals, tel (free) 0800 700740. **www.missingpersons.org**

National Council for One-Parent Families, 255 Kentish Town Road, London NW5 2LX, tel 020 7428 5400 for free information booklets for lone parents on many subjects including benefits, tax, legal rights and divorce. Helpline, tel 0800 0185 026. **www.oneparentfamilies.org.uk**

National Missing Persons Helpline 0500 700 700 provides help, information and advice to families of missing people. NMPH HQ, 284 Upper Richmond Road West, London SW14 7ZU, tel 020 8392 4590. **www.missingpersons.org**

National Society for the Prevention of Cruelty to Children (NSPCC), Weston House, 42 Curtain Road, London EC2A 3NH, tel 020 7825 2500. The NSPCC runs a free 24hr child protection helpline for children and young people, parents and anyone concerned about young people at risk, tel 0808 800 5000. **www.nspcc.org.uk**

NORCAP , 112 Church Road, Wheatley, Oxfordshire OX33 1LU, tel 01865 875 000, provides advice and support for adopted people and their birth relatives who wish to get in touch. Open Mon- Fri 10am-4.30pm. **www.norcap.org.uk**

Parentline Plus, 520 Highgate Studios, 53-79 Highgate Road, Kentish Town, London NW5 1TL, free tel 0808 800 2222, works with adults, children and young people providing information and support to families. **www.parentlineplus.org.uk**

Runaway provides a free helpline, tel 0808 800 7070, for young people under 18 who have runaway or been forced to leave home or care. Can give confidential advice, make referrals and arrange help.

Women's Aid gives information, support and advice for women experiencing domestic violence in the home. Women's Aid England run a 24 hour helpline, tel 08457 023 468. Welsh Women's Aid run a helpline, tel 01222 390874.
www.womensaid.org.uk

Home

Centrepoint, Neil House, 7 Whitechapel Road, London E1 1DU, tel 020 7426 5300, a youth homeless charity able to advise callers who have arrived in London with nowhere to stay.
www.centrepoint.org.uk

Crisis, 64 Commercial Street, London E1 1LT, tel 0870 011 33 55, email: enquiries@crisis.org.uk gives advice and assistance to homeless people.
www.crisis.org.uk

The Foyer Federation 5-9 Hatton Wall, London EC!N 8HX tel 020 7430 2212, a UK wide youth homeless charity providing accommodation, education and training opportunities for 16-25 year olds with housing needs. For details of the nearest Foyer see **www.foyer.net**

Shelter, 88 Old Street, London EC1V 9HU, campaigns to improve the housing conditions and rights of private tenants. Shelter also has a network of housing aid centres across the country and runs Shelterline, a free 24 hour national housing helpline tel 0808 800 4444.
www.shelter.org.uk

Leisure

Citizencard, PO Box 1221, Newcastle-under-Lyme ST5 0US, provide free photo-ID card and proof of age for under 18s and charge £7 for over 18s, tel, 0870 240 1221.
www.citizencard.net

Countryside Agency, John Dower House, Crescent Place, Cheltenham, Gloucestershire GL50 3RA, tel 01242 521381, for information on access and rights of way. **www.countryside.gov.uk**

Environment Agency, has offices around the country. The general enquiry line is 0845 9333 111. There is a free 24hr emergency phone line on which you can report any environmental incident, tel 0800 80 70 60.
www.environment-agency.gov.uk

Proof of Age Card Scheme, The Portman Group, 7-10 Chandos Street, Cavendish Square, London W1G 9DQ, tel 020 7907 3700. If you're 18 or over you can get a Proof of Age Card from the Portman Group for £5, call 01782 741 968, email: info@portmangroup.org.uk,
www.portman-group.org.uk

Royal Society for the Prevention of Cruelty to Animals (RSPCA), have a 24hr emergency cruelty and advice line for people who wish to report an animal in distress, tel 0870 55 55 999. For other information contact The RSPCA Enquiries Service, Wilberforce Way, Southwater, Horsham, West Sussex RH13 9RS, tel 0870 33 35 999. **www.rspca.org.uk**

Royal Society for Protection of Birds (RSPB), for advice on protected birds see **www.rspb.org.uk**

Travel and transport

ABTA (The Association of British Travel Agents), 68-71 Newman Street, London W1T 3AH, for information and advice over problems with a package holiday, tel 020 7637 2444, email: information@abta.org.uk. For general travel information, tel 0901 201 5050 (calls charged at 50p per minute). **www.abtanet.com**

Department of Transport, for information on motoring and transport law. **www.dft.gov.uk**. Enquiries 020 7944 8300. For public transport information, tel 0870 608 2608.

Driving Standards Agency, Stanley House, 56 Talbot Street, Nottingham NG1 5GU, tel 0115 901 2500 for information on driving tests for cars and compulsory basic training for motorcyclists. **www.driving-tests.co.uk**

DVLA, Licensing Centre, Longview Road, Swansea SA6 7JL, for enquiries about driving licences, tax discs or the registration details of a particular vehicle. Driver enquiries, tel 0870 240 0009; vehicle enquiries, tel 0870 240 0010. **www.dvla.gov.uk**

Euro<26 Card, see National Youth Agency site at **www.nya.org.uk/euro26**

National Express Ltd., Ensign Court, 4 Vicarage Road, Edgbaston, Birmingham B15 3ES. Information on coach travel and discount travel schemes. For telephone bookings call 0870 5 80 80 80, open every day 8am-10pm. **www.nationalexpress.com**

Royal Society for the Prevention of Accidents (RoSPA), Edgbaston Park, 353 Bristol Road, Birmingham B5 7ST, tel 0121 248 2000, email: help@rospa.com. Information on safety on the road and in the home. For a quicker reply, enclose a SAE. **www.rospa.com**

Young Persons Railcard, ATOC Ltd, 3rd Floor, 40 Bernard St., London WC1N 1BY. **www.youngpersons-railcard.co.uk**

Police and courts

Citizens Advice Bureau (CAB), have trained staff who can give free legal advice and suggest solicitors able to deal with your particular problem. See **General** section, for contact details.

The **Court Service**, Southside,105 Victoria Street, London SW1E 6QT, tel 020 7210 2266, email: cust.ser.cs@gtnet.gov.uk publishes the Courts' Charter explaining how the court system works and what you can expect if you are charged with a criminal offence or attend court as a witness, a member of a jury or as a defendant or plaintiff in a civil case. The Charter is available from your local court or CAB. **www.courtservice.gov.uk**

The **Criminal Justice System** online is at **www.cjsonline.org**

use the law with care try talking first

Legal Services Commission, Head Office, 85 Gray's Inn Road, London WC1X 8TX, tel 020 7759 0000, for information on the Community Legal Service.
www.legalservices.gov.uk.
A directory of solicitors firms able to take on criminal work is on **www.justask.org.uk**

Police Complaints Authority, 10 Great George Street, London SW1P 3AE, tel 020 7273 6450, email:info@pca.gov.uk is the official body overseeing complaints against the police. They can provide information on how to make a complaint if you have witnessed or suffered police misconduct.
www.pca.gov.uk

Law, government and human rights

POLITICAL PARTIES

Conservative Party, 32 Smith Square, London SW1P 3HH, tel 020 7222 9000.
www.conservatives.com

Green Party, 1a Waterlow Road, London N19 5NJ, tel 020 7272 4474.
www.greenparty.org.uk

Labour Party, 16 Old Queen St, London SW1H 9HP, tel 08705 900 200.
www.labour.org.uk

Liberal Democrats, 4 Crowley St., London SW1P 3DH, tel 020 7222 7999.
www.libdems.org.uk

Plaid Cymru, the Party of Wales, Ty Gwynfor, 18 Park Grove, Cardiff CF1 3BN, tel 029 2064 6000.
www.plaidcymru.org.

GENERAL

House of Commons Information Office, House of Commons, London SW1A 0AA, tel 020 7219 3000. A public information service on the working and proceedings of Parliament. **www.parliament.uk**

For information on the **Human Rights Act**, refer to the Department for Constitutional Affairs website **www.dca.gov.uk/hract**

The European Union

The Council of Europe, an organisation with a strong interest in human rights, which works to find solutions to some of the problems facing European society, Avenue de L'Europe, 67075 Strasbourg Cedex, France, tel +33(0)3 88 41 20 33, email: infopoint@coe.int; **www.coe.int**

European Commission, can indicate your nearest centre for information, tel 020 7973 1992. Representation in the UK, 8 Storey's Gate, London, SW1P 3AT, tel 020 7973 1900. **www.cec.org.uk**

European Parliament Information Office, 2 Queen Anne's Gate, London SW1H 9AA, tel 020 7227 4300.em eplondon@europarl.eu.int For a free information service on the European Parliament, tel 00 800 678 91011:
www.europarl.org.uk

European Youth Forum (EYF), represents youth organisations from all over Europe.
www.youthforum.org.

Organising Bureau of School Students Unions (OBESSU), tel +32(0) 264 72 390, email: obessu@obessu.org, coordinates national organisations of schools and provides European representation for school students. **www.obessu.org.**